The Man Who Restored Pride

by

David J. Mooney

Best wishes

The Man Who
Restored Pride

by

David J. Mooney

Published in the United Kingdom by Jiggery Pokery 2013.

First published in the United Kingdom in 2013 by Jiggery Pokery.

http://www.davemooney.co.uk
http://www.twitter.com/DavidMooney

ISBN: 978-0-9573113-1-2

Printed and bound by CPI Group (UK) Ltd, Croydon, CR0 4YY

For Helen and Dave

Acknowledgements

Special thanks to Helen and Dave Mooney for their support; to Gary James for his help and advice; Kev Robinson for editing this book; Adam Carter for allowing me access to his statistical data; Niall Taylor and Karl Florczak for use of photographs they've taken; Dave and Sue Wallace for their work in producing *King of the Kippax* and publishing my articles in the magazine; Chris Prince, Dan Burns and Richard Burns (who is no relation to the former) for their work on *Blue Moon Live*; to Paul Atherton, Sam Rosbottom and Howard Hockin for their contributions to the *Blue Moon Podcast*; Tom Greggan for his City trivia knowledge; and Paul Sarahs for sparking ideas through Twitter conversations about City.

About the Author

David J. Mooney got his first season ticket for Manchester City in 1997. Despite not witnessing much in the way of success on the pitch, he continued to go and eventually saw the club play in the same division in consecutive seasons for the first time in 2003.

He began to write about football while he was studying journalism at university, producing articles on a manner of subjects for various blogs and websites. It was also at this time that he started to submit material to *King of the Kippax*, where he was able to develop his voice, while expressing his opinions about the club he loved.

In 2009, having finished university and while looking to break into radio journalism, he founded *The Blue Moon Podcast* and has hosted, produced and edited the show since. He was then invited to be on the panel on *BlueMoon Live*, a new Manchester City live show on *Imagine FM* in 2010, which he has also gone on to host and produce.

Following City's title win in 2012, David produced his first paperback football book based on the club since the takeover in 2008. *Typical City* looked back at every game the blues had played in the four years leading up to being crowned Champions, including various articles he'd written and interviews he'd done over that time.

Now in his mid-twenties, he's given up on his dream of keeping goal for City and is now content to do it on a Wednesday evening at a local five-a-side centre.

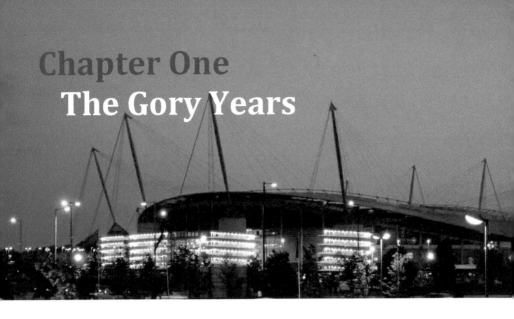

Chapter One
The Gory Years

MANCHESTER CITY HAS NEVER BEEN a football club to support if you suffer from any kind of medical condition. In fact, should there ever be a need to properly formalise the whole process and fill in a fan application form, the club will surely be turning down people in high volumes because of pre-existing heart conditions or traumas experienced earlier in life. Supporting City creates so many health problems in itself that it would be too dangerous to take anybody who isn't in peak physical condition.

While some teams have been able to enjoy relative stability, few will be able to boast that a mere 14 years after having recorded their lowest ever league position they have won the top division title in this country. For the record, that's not actually following the club's defeat to York in December 1998 – that left the Blues a mere 12th in Division Two. Earlier that season, a 1-1 draw at Notts County plunged the club down to 14th position, 58 places below then Premier League leaders Aston Villa (yes, you read that correctly, though the fact the top division had only played three games by this point probably has a lot to do with who occupied its summit).

And to have won the top division from such a low point in just 14 years, it would be reasonable to expect some sort of progress season by season. But that's not really the Manchester City way. No, City don't really do steady building blocks. They prefer a rollercoaster that the health and safety people would more than likely close down due to the high volume of complaints of serious whiplash. In the time between that lowest ebb and the 2012 title win, City fans witnessed six new managers, three promotions, a relegation, two high profile takeovers, three near financial meltdowns, four trips to Wembley, two years of finishing in the top three, four UEFA Cup or Europa League exits and one Christian Negouai.

Manchester City 2-2 Gillingham
Sunday 30 May 1999
Division Two Playoff Final

City: Weaver, Crooks (G Taylor 85), Edghill, Wiekens, Morrison (c) (Vaughan 61), Horlock, Brown (Bishop 61), Whitley, Dickov, Goater, Cooke
Goals: Horlock (90), Dickov (90+5)

Following the Full Members' Cup final in 1986, City fans probably weren't expecting to wait 13 years for their next trip to Wembley – and even then, they'd have probably been expecting it in different circumstances. A promotion push was just too late, meaning they faced the playoffs. And, at the end of May, the fans headed south.

Having been on top throughout the match, City found themselves two behind with three minutes to play. Horlock and Dickov saved the day and, with neither side able to win in extra time, it went to penalties. Spot kicks from Horlock, Cooke and Edghill (and saves from Weaver) won out.

And this is where the rise to the top started. Fourteen years before winning the title, the very future of the club was saved in dramatic style. It's hardly surprising how they won the Premier League.

To provide further insight into how violent the twists and turns on this rollercoaster were, you need look no further than Christian Negouai himself. He was a man who will not be known to most football supporters outside of the City fanbase, but he was the perfect metaphor for how eventful things were at the club in such a short space of time.

Signed by Kevin Keegan, Negouai cost the club £1.5m – a fee that was clearly buttons in comparison to the level of entertainment he brought. In his first game at Maine Road, he endeared himself to the fans with a spectacularly blatant (yet somehow missed by the officials) 'hand of God goal', as he punched the ball into the Rotherham net. In his four years with the club, he made 10 appearances – four of which were starts and only two of which were starts in the league – and scored two goals.

Christian Negouai
Born: 20 Jan 1978
Signed: 13 Nov 2001
Sold: 7 Jul 2005
Apps: 4 (6 sub)
Goals: 2
Yellow Cards: 1
Red Cards: 2
Notes: Held the record for the fastest Premier League sending off after coming on as a substitute (3 minutes).

But that wasn't it for Negouai, who seemed to be surrounded by controversy. A red card in his third start for the club (this one coming in a League Cup tie at Blackburn) arrived in comical fashion. On a wet evening where the conditions weren't ideal for diving into challenges, referee Uriah Rennie flashed two yellow cards in his direction in a mere 26 minutes for two trademark Negouai lunges.

Following the Blues' promotion to the Premier League at the end of Negouai's first season with the club, he seemingly disappeared off the radar, as a series of injuries hampered his progress. Following that red card at Blackburn, he made just one more appearance in two and a half years, scoring in his solitary start against TNS at the

Millennium Stadium. Before he left in 2005, he managed to play 13 minutes of a League Cup tie against Arsenal (coming on and later going off as a substitute) and featured in three Premier League minutes – coming off the bench on 80 minutes against Everton, before being sent back to the bench on 83 minutes for a straight red card on a foul on Marcus Bent.

All of that came in just ten appearances, spanning 373 minutes and four seasons.

And it's for this reason why Negouai sums up City from those 14 years, as so much was crammed into so little time. The year with Sven in charge saw City transform from a relegation-threatened team to one capable of challenging for the Champions League to one putting up little fight against finishing in mid-table, all over the course of 38 games. And all that happened only four years before the club lifted the title.

Joe Mercer
13 Jul 1965 – 7 Oct 1971

Played: 337
Won: 150
Drawn: 92
Lost: 95

Goals For: 525
Goals Against: 361

Win Rate: 44.51%

It's easy to refer to the Mercer-Allison time at City as the 'glory years' given the successes the club had on the pitch. Trophies were regularly adorning the cabinet at Maine Road, while the football on show was a joy to watch. If those were the 'glory years', it would seem appropriate to rename the period of about 1996 to 2009 as the 'gory years', as the fans observed crisis after embarrassment after cock-up after shambles. It wasn't a pleasant sight.

There's often been a certain sympathy about City fans when they witness other clubs' downfalls. Obviously it's a feeling that comes rivalry aside (I daresay there's a fair few

Blues out there who would take great delight in witnessing some of the club's rivals slip down the league table) but, on the whole, when the fans see others going through the 'what is happening to us?' phase, they understand the pain. Helpless, we know all too well how it feels to be able to do nothing to stop the self-destruct button being pushed.

After all, when it comes to stability, City have been on a par with a plutonium rod balanced on some jelly in a wind tunnel. That's to say they've been mostly shaky, often causing a state of confusion for onlookers, and occasionally seen in fluorescent colours – yes, 2005-2007 bright yellow third shirt, I'm looking at you, and I am also nodding in your direction, 2008-2009 bright orange debacle.

Premier League Managers By Game

Roberto Mancini: 133
Kevin Keegan: 105
Stuart Pearce: 85
Brian Horton: 79
Mark Hughes: 55
Peter Reid: 46
Alan Ball: 38
Sven Goran Eriksson: 38
Joe Royle: 38

The very fact that Roberto Mancini, in his third full season in charge, became City's longest serving Premier League manager tells the story. Chopping and changing is something the club has down to a tee, with Kevin Keegan's 105 top flight games eclipsed by the Italian's 133.

In the past, though, as managers have changed, there's been the general sense of reason behind the decision. It's been a decision that has often split the fans, but, in the end, the split was big enough to say that it was more than just a couple of dissenting voices. Even in the days when Sven Goran Eriksson was sacked, there was a decent argument for it happening, given the awful form the team had shown in the second half of the season.

Still, it seems odd, however, that the Blues would choose to sack a manager who was bringing silverware to the club. Ok, so the 2012-13 season ended with City having only won the Community Shield (and it's coming to something when we're saying "only won the Community Shield" given the previous four decades), but this was the first dip in Roberto Mancini's tenure. He'd shown improvement in every year and, in his first two full campaigns, delivered a trophy in each.

And yet the axe still fell.

Why not go for stability? Why not stick with the man who was, by and large, producing results on the pitch? Why not make sure that there is regularity in the control of the squad – especially given how Mancini had become the City manager with the most Premier League matches? Maybe stability isn't always the best answer and maybe a lot of fans were too quick to dismiss rumours about what was happening away from the pitch. Stability would do no good in a situation where things aren't going right.

What would have happened, for example, if the club had stuck by Mark Hughes for the sake of stability? Or if John Wardle had decided to keep things the same at board level in order to avoid disrupting the fragile nature of the club, despite the dire financial situation at the time? It's all hypothetical, of course, but with every decision that could alter the future of a football team, there is the huge risk that it won't pay off.

For the gory years, it didn't pay off for City. Again, not necessarily proving that stability in the management was key, though – because what's the point in sticking by a man who wasn't getting results (and I could be talking about numerous managers here)? It's no good avoiding disrupting the balance of the club if the wrong people are in the wrong jobs, be it they're the right person at the wrong time or the wrong person altogether.

It's clear the board at City had no intentions of sacking Mancini at the start of the season – after all, they wouldn't have negotiated a five year contract with a man they knew they'd be relieving of his duties in the near future. So clearly there was a long-term plan with him at the helm.

Though, with the performances hitting a below par standard, City's falling short of their expectations in all of the competitions they entered, plus regular stories of malcontent and disharmony behind the scenes, it's also clear to see why the board felt concerned over whether that long-term plan was being met and, if not, whether it ever would be.

The fans that called for stability had been influenced by the continued successes the club had experienced on the pitch since Mancini took charge and it was difficult not to be. Indeed, I was one who had the opinion that he shouldn't have been sacked, given he had achieved second place in the league and reached a cup final, on top of his previous seasons. Though I – and the majority of others – didn't know what was going on behind the scenes.

The Roberto Mancini years were eventful, both in matches and away from them. And, in the context of everything that had gone before during the previous 14 years, it was fully understandable why he had such a good relationship with the fans – the very fact the man himself and the supporters exchanged adverts in each other's local newspaper thanking the other for what they had done speaks volumes.

Slowly but surely, though, things went wrong for Mancini. Not that that means the memories should be devalued, far from it – they were some of the best times the club has enjoyed. However, it can just go to show that, even during the best of times and the worst of times, Manchester City will never change.

And that's a blessing – because life supporting a regular football club would be just so boring, right?

Chapter Two
As Good As It Gets

"**Y**OU'RE NOT FIT TO WEAR the shirt!"

Stuart Pearce must have been wondering where it had all gone wrong. In May of 2005 he was within a penalty kick of securing European football for Manchester City through league position rather than through UEFA's Fair Play League. It would have been a step above his predecessor, Kevin Keegan. Two years on, however, the honeymoon period was a distant memory, as 7000 fans shouted abuse at the players and management team from the Darwen End of Ewood Park. It's one thing to lose. It's another to put in a display that lacked heart, passion, fighting spirit, or even effort.

Manchester City had been dumped out of the FA Cup at the quarter final stage by a ten-man Blackburn Rovers side. For yet another season, the dream of silverware was gone. And that match was a tipping point for a lot of Blues fans.

Sunday 11 March 2007 saw perhaps one of the most vocal protests from supporters in the trophy barren spell; one angry fan had to be dragged away from the dugout after venting his annoyance directly at Pearce, having run onto the Blackburn pitch in sheer frustration at the end of

Blackburn Rovers 2-0 Manchester City
Sunday 11 March 2007, FA Cup Quarter Final

City: Weaver, Richards, Dunne (c), Distin, Jihai (Beasley 57), Barton, Hamann (Samaras 76), Ireland, Ball, Corradi (Mpenza 81), Vassell
Goals: -

Having struggled all season in the league, City travelled to Blackburn in their toughest draw of the FA Cup run so far in 2007. After scraping past Sheffield Wednesday, the Blues beat Southampton and Preston North End to take their place in the quarter final. The cup, once again, represented their best shot at silverware, as the years rolled by since Dennis Tueart's 1976 overhead kick.

But City's performance was spineless and, despite starting the better, there soon appeared to be only one winner. The very fact that Blackburn had a man sent off after 69 minutes and that it made no difference to the outcome summed up the lack of passion in the visiting team.

It was this game that made the future look nothing but bleak for the fans and the frustrations boiled over on that spring evening.

the game. Another made a beeline for then captain Richard Dunne, who was one of the few players that season who seemingly cared about the future of the club.

As the players left the pitch the TV cameras were focused on the away end – and it wasn't a pretty sight. The collective mass of fans had been pushed to breaking point and the chants towards anybody who was even vaguely connected with Manchester City were filled with a new level of pure, unadulterated rage. A lack of success had been commonplace and supporters, while not being overly happy about it, had accepted that progress takes time and rebuilding a club that was at its lowest ever point less than a decade earlier would have no quick fix. But this was beginning to feel like the result of another in a long chain of bad decisions: it's hard to take having your hopes continually dashed and the City fans were showing it.

I watched that game in a pub in Preston, where I was in my first year of university. There were four of us in the group watching the football and I was the only member who wasn't impartial. City's trip to Blackburn was the first game being shown, with the second match that evening seeing Watford travel to Plymouth. We drew a sweepstake for teams to qualify for the next round: whoever's team won would get half the pot. I drew Manchester City.

At the final whistle, as tensions ran high, thoughts gradually turned away from the FA Cup defeat to the bleakness of the future. Having lost in the League Cup to Chesterfield earlier in the season, there were now only 11 Premier League fixtures left for the club. And, with the Blues in 17th place, below them were just three teams: West Ham, Watford and Charlton. Only Watford had scored fewer goals, with City having found the net (on average) once every 121 minutes.

The word 'bleak' actually seems too mild for the situation the club was in.

In truth, relegation fears were quickly eased. Directly following that FA Cup exit, the Blues lost at home to Chelsea, but then took ten points from their next four games and went unbeaten in five, as a good Easter period propelled the club to safety. By the end of the season, lower-mid-table obscurity had set in, and, having nothing to play for, they had slipped to 14th.

Despite easing to safety, the general consensus around the City of Manchester Stadium was that the club was heading in the wrong direction. Again.

I don't remember much of Watford's 1-0 victory over Plymouth that evening. Just like the fans at Ewood Park, I

Manchester City 1-2 West Ham United
Monday 20 March 2006
FA Cup Quarter Final

City: James, Richards, Dunne, Distin (c), Jordan (Sommeil 24), Jihai, Barton (Ireland 79), Musampa, Riera, Vassell, Wright-Phillips (Croft 73)
Goals: Musampa (85)
Sent Off: Jihai

City fans were getting excited. It had been 25 years since their club had graced the FA Cup semi final and they were quietly confident that this could be their year. A congested fixture list – this the club's second of three games in seven days – didn't help and a depleted squad made matters worse, as Samaras became the latest to limp off injured two days earlier against Wigan.

A dubious second goal and an equally unfortunate red card left City with little hope, despite a late Musampa volley. The FA Cup semi final wait would have to go on for at least another season.

was in shock. In the years before – while Keegan was manager, while the club was still at Maine Road, while Joe Royle was earning two promotions in a row – there was always hope for the future. There were signs things, both on and off the pitch, were improving. There were promotions. There was a quality of football that was easy on the eye. There were signings that brought with them a new level of excitement and all of which felt like a coup for the club. There was a move to a new stadium to look forward to.

But all that had gone and, in the evening of Sunday 11 March 2007, I came to the conclusion that this was as good as it was ever going to get to be a City fan. The season before, the club had been knocked out of the FA Cup at the same stage, losing to West Ham at Eastlands. Then, though, there were mitigating circumstances: a harsh red card for Sun Jihai and a goal that was questionably offside had given the club an uphill battle that they just couldn't overcome.

This time it was purely City's fault: they didn't match up to Blackburn on any level.

With the club strapped for cash and with few signs of that changing, it dawned on me during that second FA Cup tie that a quarter final of a domestic cup and Premier League survival would probably be the best I could hope for. This could quite conceivably sound like I'd not have been thankful to be watching Premier League football – there are teams that have this aspect of the game as just a dream, after all – however, that's not the case. It's just (for want of a better word) boring: the relegation threat would leave mid-April, there'd be the odd memorable win and devastating loss, but little else. For those dreaming of better things below, there is always the chance that dream could be realised, just like as has happened to clubs like Swansea or Blackpool in recent seasons. This felt like City had come as far as they physically could and the dream was over.

Yet football fandom is like a religion. One is devoted to it and, no matter what happens, that never changes. Just ten league goals at home all season, uninspiring football and being embarrassed regularly did little to change my opinion that, yes, I would indeed like to renew my season ticket. Many didn't at the end of that campaign – and that tells you just how bad it was getting.

Here's how I saw the future: Stuart Pearce would lose his job; his mediocre set of players would be replaced by the next manager's mediocre set of players; the club would enjoy a pick-me-up under the new boss, but two years

Stuart Pearce

11 Mar 2005 – 14 May 2007

PL Played: 85
PL Won: 28
PL Drawn: 17
PL Lost: 40

PL Goals For: 85
PL Goals Against: 99

PL Win Rate: 32.94%

or so on it would have all turned sour; and repeat. Best-case scenario, nothing would happen. Worst-case, another relegation.

Perhaps that wouldn't have been so bad, given what the fans had to deal with next.

It had all seemed rosy at the start of the following year. The good mood that had enveloped the club when Stuart Pearce began in 2005 was back, as a close season takeover from the former Thai Prime Minister Thaksin Shinawatra had brought several brand new exciting signings and an internationally renowned manager in Sven Goran Eriksson. Collectively, fans had had their heads turned by attractive football – something they had been starved of for a long time – and a run of victories. A first home goal in the league in eight months was enough to see off Derby, before Manchester United were dispatched by the same 1-0 scoreline in the third game of the season.

Excitement was running high as, at Christmas, the Blues were still in the top four and unbeaten at home – dropping just four points by the turn of the year, as Liverpool and Blackburn had left Eastlands with draws. Maybe this

Premier League Table
23 December 2007

		W	D	L	Pts
1	Arsenal	13	4	1	43
2	Man Utd	13	3	2	42
3	Chelsea	11	4	3	37
4	Man City	10	4	4	34

was the year that the club could actually qualify for Europe – be it the UEFA Cup or the Champions League – through finishing inside the top six, something that hadn't been done in decades.

Maybe not.

City don't really do false dawns softly. From January onwards, the Blues won just five times in the final half of the season. In fact, it would be very fair to say the form

Manchester United 1-2 Manchester City
Sunday 10 February 2008, Premier League

City: Hart, Onuoha, Richards, Dunne (c), Ball, Vassell, Ireland, Hamann (Jihai 84), Gelson, Petrov (Garrido 87), Benjani (Caicedo 75)
Goals: Vassell (25), Benjani (45)

Perhaps this match was City's performance of the season, though few fans were expecting what they saw in February 2008. It was United's memorial for the 50th anniversary of the Munich air disaster and special kits were worn for the occasion. It was a Manchester derby and the script was written for the Reds to beat the Blues.

But Sven's City had other ideas and they weren't just victorious, but they were the better team throughout. Goals from Vassell and Benjani were enough to win the match, though there were plenty more chances for the visitors to have extended their lead and Hart's goal was rarely threatened. For a generation, Sven was the first City manager to beat United on their own patch.

book wasn't just torn up, but rather burnt to cinders, as the club slid out of the top four, through the top six and down into 9th, finishing the campaign with a negative goal difference.

A first derby double in over 30 years did nothing to ease the pain of a final day 8-1 thrashing at Middlesbrough. Goal after goal after goal hit the back of Andreas Isaksson's net and, as I headed out of the living room in my house where Sky Sports News was telling me the worsening scoreline and into my bedroom where I started

Darius Vassell

Born: 30 Jun 1980
Signed: 27 Jul 2005
Sold: 1 Jul 2009

Apps: 110 (14 sub)
Goals: 22
Yellow Cards: 14
Red Cards: 0
Notes: Never lost a Premier League match in which he'd scored.

up my PlayStation, I thought back to that day in the pub. Despite the buoyant mood at City at the start of the 2007-08 season, we were right back where we had started – a mediocre mid-table club, with a manager employing tactics that did little to change the club's fortunes.

Sven had told the press that his tactics had been "found out", yet he persited with the same set-up each match. Injuries to his defence did take their toll – towards the end of the season, City's back four was made up of three full backs and Elano, a creative midfielder – but there was little to inspire confidence for the fans from any other part of the team.

I didn't find out the final score of City's trip to Teesside until the next day, when the thought occurred that the Blues may have qualified for Europe via the Fair Play League. Again.

It had been another difficult end to the season. Leaks from within the club

---

Middlesbrough 8-1 Manchester City
Sunday 11 May 2008, Premier League

City: Isaksson, Jihai, Corluka, Dunne (c), Ball, Ireland, Gelson, Petrov (Elano 71), Garrido, Vassell (Hamann 62), Benjani (Castillo 13)
Goals: Elano (87)
Sent Off: Dunne

There are several theories as to why this result was as bad as it was. Perhaps it was a protest about the leaked stories that Sven was to lose his job. Perhaps it was a team devoid of spirit because their manager had been undermined. Perhaps it was none of those reasons; perhaps it was just one atrocious display lacking in heart, fight or desire.

Either way, it resulted in a game where Adam Johnson would score against his future club, Alfonso Alves scored a hat-trick and Middlesbrough scored over three goals in a game for the first time all season. In the end, it was a mere footnote that City had qualified for the UEFA Cup at the final whistle.

---

had suggested Sven would lose his job at the end of the campaign and, for the most part, it had the fans in uproar, many of which agreed that the quality of the start to his City career had demonstrated enough to suggest he should be allowed another year to turn it around. The same fans demanding change a year earlier were now demanding stability.

Despite the *Save Our Sven* campaign, the chairman relieved the Swede of his duties.

The cycle started again as Mark Hughes took over the reigns. Except, this time, there was no lift to kick the season off. The fans had seen it all before and, being truthful, it was becoming quite tiresome. The club was back in its rut, though this time there was complete financial oblivion on the horizon – and it wasn't just media hyperbole. It was so real, in fact, that there was talk of Vedran Corluka being sold behind the manager's back to raise funds.

Sven Goran Eriksson
6 Jul 2007 – 2 Jun 2008

PL Played: 38
PL Won: 15
PL Drawn: 10
PL Lost: 13

PL Goals For: 45
PL Goals Against: 53

PL Win Rate: 39.47%

Before the final pre-season friendly with AC Milan, Stephen Ireland was told he was being sold to Sunderland, again unbeknownst to Mark Hughes, who quickly got on the phone half an hour before kick-off to tell the midfielder he was required for first team duty. A group of former directors had got together in secret, ready to buy the club should they get into a situation where only a rescue package would save them. Something was clearly very wrong.

However, some exciting news for the fans emerged on transfer deadline day. The day that began with Corluka joining Tottenham ended with the Blues being dubbed 'the richest club in the world', following the second takeover in as many years. Sheikh Mansour bin Zayed bin Sultan Al Nahyan had bought out the controversial Thaksin Shinawatra and, as a statement of intent, the club secured the signature of the Real Madrid forward and Chelsea target Robinho. Things were suddenly looking up.

Come Christmas Day, City were in the relegation zone, following a 2-1 defeat to West Brom at The Hawthorns. The year before, the club had been sitting pretty in fourth – 2008 was definitely not kind

Premier League Table
22 December 2008

		W	D	L	Pts
17	West Ham	5	4	9	19
18	Man City	5	3	10	18
19	Blackburn	4	4	10	16
20	West Brom	4	3	11	15

to the Blues. Performances were worse than ever – arguably worse than when Pearce's City whimpered to Premier League survival. Turmoil would be an understatement, as one step forward was followed by four or five backwards and signings made that following January were aimed at keeping the club in the division, rather than finalising a push for Europe as the new chairman had hoped. Many speculated that the only thing keeping Mark Hughes in a job was City's performances in the UEFA Cup.

Though losing to Hamburg in another quarter final was disappointing, this time there was, at least, the comfort that the players on the pitch had given their all.

Stephen Ireland

Born: 22 Aug 1986
Signed: Academy, 2005
Sold: 18 Aug 2010

Apps: 142 (34 sub)
Goals: 23
Yellow Cards: 12
Red Cards: 1
Notes: Showed underpants when he scored against Sunderland.

This was a cup knockout that was purely down to a lack of quality, rather than a lack of effort, too. While upsetting, fans will always forgive players not being good enough, but they will never forget somebody who doesn't try.

By the end of the season, the club had finished lower than they did the previous year. They had won just two of 19 away games. They had been knocked out of both domestic cups by lower league opposition in the shape of Brighton and Nottingham Forest. There was no drubbing on the final day of the season, though it was obvious a lot of changes were needed for the club to have any thoughts of improving to a standard deemed sufficient by chairman Khaldoon Al Mubarak.

> **Robinho**
>
> **Born:** 25 Jan 1984
> **Signed:** 1 Sep 2008
> **Sold:** 31 Aug 2010
>
> **Apps:** 48 (5 sub)
> **Goals:** 16
> **Yellow Cards:** 4
> **Red Cards:** 0
> **Notes:** Scored three quarters of his City goals at Eastlands.

By this stage, I had graduated from university. Despite having gone through internal changes as huge as physically possible for a football club during my time in higher education, Manchester City couldn't have been more the same if they had tried. Each year, there was a different manager. Each year, there was a different set of players. Yet each year, the club ended up in mid-table and was knocked out in a cup quarter final – be it the FA Cup (2006-07), the League Cup (2007-08) or the UEFA Cup (2008-09).

No matter what happened at Manchester City, it seemed I was right.

This actually was as good as it was ever going to get.

Chapter Three
The Changing of the Guard

OPTIMISM WAS ALWAYS SOMETHING THAT was unusual for City fans. If there ever was a time when confidence was sweeping through the supporters, there were more than a couple looking over their shoulders for the knife that would inevitably smash through their shoulder blades. The feeling that 'anything that can go wrong, will go wrong' was always perceived from the outside as gallows humour, or something Blues did because they were lurking around the nether regions of the Football League. And while I'm sure that was at least partly the case, few will deny that, in the pits of their stomachs, they always knew City were capable of messing everything up. City do optimism about as well as I do nuclear physics.

Being confident when City are involved has always – but always – bitten fans on the backside. Do you ever feel comfortable when two goals up against Fulham, for example? How frequently have you uttered the words 'potential banana skin' when the cup draw has seen City travel to a lower league ground? Just who exactly is a sending off supposed to benefit, given the number of times City have lost to ten men? Confidence is a new thing for the fans – certainly the younger ones, anyway.

So, when the summer of 2009 rocks up and the Blues bring in eight new faces, including the likes of Gareth Barry, Kolo Toure and Emmanuel Adebayor, a strange sense of optimism filled the mentality of the fans. Nevermind anymore that, the season before, the club had won two away games all campaign, finished lower than the year before and had spent Christmas in the relegation zone. That didn't matter – City had become one of the most exciting prospects in the Premier League and a top four finish was on the cards.

Having started brightly at Ewood Park, City went on to win the next three games of the season. Of the four opening victories, three of them were to nil. Sandwiched in the middle was a League Cup win over Crystal Palace. In fact, in competitive football, by the time Robin van Persie equalised for Arsenal in City's 4-2 win, the Blues had gone eight hours, 36 minutes since conceding their last goal – scored by Robbie Keane at White Hart Lane in the penultimate game of 2008-09.

Talk about a boost to an already cautiously confident fanbase.

This meant that, when travelling to Old Trafford in the fifth league game of the season, there was the general sense of optimism that the Blues could repeat their trick of February 2008 and win. Despite being on the back foot for large spells of the game, City dug deep and hit back whenever United took the lead, scoring equalisers through Gareth Barry and two from Craig Bellamy, the last looking like it had rescued a point.

Obviously, we all know better, as referee Martin Atkinson kept playing, while City stopped and Michael Owen strolled unmarked through the box to win it in the sixth of five added minutes of stoppage time. However, that sense of injustice did something to the fans' mentality: it

Manchester United 4-3 Manchester City
Sunday 20 September 2009, Premier League

City: Given, Richards, Bridge, Lescott, Toure (c), Ireland, Wright-Phillips, Barry, de Jong (Petrov 83), Tevez, Bellamy
Goals: Barry (16), Bellamy (52, 90)

The first Manchester derby of the 2009-10 season was seen as a benchmark as to how far City had come since the takeover. The club had won all of their games so far that season and they were pushing for honours at the top end of the Premier League, so there's a sense of irony that this game represented the start of the slide for Mark Hughes. After losing in the last minute at Old Trafford, he'd go on to win just two more league matches at City, losing one and drawing eight.

And, while the manner of the defeat was difficult to swallow, perhaps it was one of the best things that could have happened to City. It exposed defensive weaknesses that had previously not been tested and needed fixing. Yet, it gave the club and the fans a sense of hope and realisation that they had progressed a long way, being able to push United to that late stage in the game at Old Trafford before losing. Though it was still a bitter pill, with the goal coming after the point when the final whistle should have sounded.

galvanised it. City had played so well and had the game snatched from them unfairly; if this is how well they can play against the reigning champions and away from home too, then imagine how well the rest of the season could go. They'd be a shoe-in for a top four spot.

Following the victory over West Ham the week later, City had won five out of their six league matches. That number of wins, though, remained at five for another seven fixtures, as the Blues broke the record for the number of consecutive Premier League draws.

And, as those draws racked up, the season's initial optimism seeped into nervousness. The record was ever looming. Draw after draw was notched up and that nervousness turned into concern: things should have been going better. Something in the region of £120m had been spent on improving the team over the summer, yet clubs that would go on to be relegated later that season had come to Eastlands and taken away a point. In fact, of those seven draws, four came against teams that finished in the bottom half of the table and three of them were at home.

That isn't the form of a Champions League chasing side and the initial confidence had drained away. The club that always bites back had bitten back.

In many ways, it was an odd feeling to be a fan in the final stages of Mark Hughes' reign. It was the first time in a long time that the club's financial future was secure. Under Stuart Pearce, it was painfully obvious given the level of investment in the team that there was little in the way of funds available for the manager, while a potential fire sale of first team players behind the manager's back after the first season under Thaksin Shinawatra was a worrying sign. As has been reported since, there was a group of former board members who were ready to put a package together to save Manchester City FC, should it be needed, as more and more

Mark Hughes
4 Jun 2008 – 19 Dec 2009

PL Played: 55
PL Won: 22
PL Drawn: 13
PL Lost: 20

PL Goals For: 91
PL Goals Against: 77

PL Win Rate: 40.00%

of the former Thai prime minister's assets were frozen.

Yet despite the financial security afforded by the ownership of Sheikh Mansour, there were clearly underlying problems in the team and perhaps even the club. There appeared to be the belief that, while City were a team in the midst of a progression from a mid-table to a top four side, the hard work would take care of itself. There was a new quality running through the squad that hadn't been there in recent seasons, yet the hunger and passion that had seen the side perform somewhat successfully (especially in the early days under Pearce and Keegan) had gone, replaced with a complacency that the team was better than their opposition. Technically, they were; but they dropped a lot of points by not turning up.

> **Carlos Tevez**
>
> **Born:** 5 Feb 1984
> **Signed:** 14 Jul 2009
> **Sold:** -
>
> **Apps:** 125 (23 sub)
> **Goals:** 74
> **Yellow Cards:** 20
> **Red Cards:** 0
> **Notes:** Up to the end of 2012-13, only ever scored one goal in a City defeat.

Spurs away, I'm looking at you.

Something needed to change. With regular below-par performances, questions started to be raised of the management team. It was one thing to be losing or drawing matches with moments of bad luck, but this wasn't the case. There was poor defending, schoolboy mistakes, and, worst of all, players who looked as if they didn't give a flying fart whether the game ended in victory or defeat. The unrest was beginning to become understandable, as this was another case of fans finding it difficult to forgive an apparent lack of effort on the pitch. More so when it became clear Mark Hughes didn't believe the side were doing much wrong, still insisting that bad luck and individual errors were a large slice of the problem.

The worry was when it seemed like he had no plan to change the team's fortunes.

In December 2009, Roberto Mancini took charge of the vacant manager's position, following the sacking of Mark Hughes shortly after the final whistle of the 4-3 home win over Sunderland. Symptomatic of Hughes' time in charge of the Blues, his final three games saw the club win one, lose one and draw one, conceding three in each (drawing 3-3 with Bolton, losing 3-0 to Tottenham and winning 4-3 against Sunderland). The very fact City could have scored three goals in each of those matches and still only taken one more point than they did says a lot about the defensive understanding the team had. In the first 17 games of 2009-10 (those managed by Hughes), the club conceded 27 goals, compared to 18 in the final 21 games under Mancini.

2009-10 PL Record

Mark Hughes
P17 W7 D8 L2 F33 A27
Win Rate: 41.18%
Clean Sheets: 4
Biggest Win: 4-2
Heaviest Loss: 3-0

Roberto Mancini
P21 W11 D5 L4 F40 A18
Win Rate: 52.38%
Clean Sheets: 7
Biggest Win: 6-1
Heaviest Loss: 0-2

While the change in manager divided the fans at the time, towards the end of the season it was beginning to look like a situation where many would regret not the decision, but the manner in which it was executed. The fact that Hughes left the pitch against Sunderland seemingly knowing he'd lost his job, plus the farce that followed in Mancini's first press conference resulted in something of a difficult transition. That said, you'd have never guessed looking at the results, as Mancini won four of his first five games, conceding in just two of them.

Immediately, the defensive fragility had gone. The very same players that had appeared as stable as a Jeremy Kyle guest who had just been found out to have cheated on their partner, now looked like they knew what they were doing. Several of those defenders, in fact, went on to become regular members of City's title winning team some two and a half seasons later.

Initially, Mancini's methods had seemed somewhat unorthodox. There were leaks to the press that players were unhappy with double training sessions, some feeling overworked in the week before matches. The Italian's tactical switches appeared to take some fans by surprise

Zonal Marking

There are two styles of marking when defending set pieces, with each having its own positives and negatives. One of the first moves Roberto Mancini made when he joined City was to switch from a man marking system to a zonal marking system, where attacking players were allowed to roam free inside the penalty. The theory was simple – providing everybody did their job correctly, when the ball came into the box, it would land near to a City player because each of them had been assigned a section of the area to cover. If it arrived in their zone, their job was to get it clear.

Its major criticism was simple, too. Players holding position in their zones were defending with a static start – a standing jump. Any attacker running in to meet a cross would be able to use their momentum to climb higher and win the ball. However, there would, in theory, be a challenge, while when man-marking, runs can be difficult to track.

Critics of the zonal system seemed to have one main argument, which involved being able to know who failed when a man marking defence conceded a goal. However, Mancini clearly preferred his defensive set-up to be based on what worked for his team, rather than how easy it was to blame somebody afterwards. After all, in both systems, the outcome is the same if a player doesn't do what they should.

too, leaving many scratching their heads over what the manager had seen and what he was trying the achieve. It was an uncomfortable end of the season, as speculation continued that he was simply a stopgap until the club could sign another manager in the summer, and, on the pitch, the all-out attacking flair had been replaced by a cautious approach, designed on keeping possession of the ball.

Little did we know at the time that this was Mancini laying down the foundations on which he would build his title winning side of 2012. He drummed it into the team that percentage balls were not worth playing; fans who were used to seeing wide players cross the ball rather than cut inside found it odd, but to Mancini the principle was simple: a pass to feet would drag the opposition defence out of position and keep the ball in the Blues' possession, while a cross into the box gives defenders the chance to win the ball back. There's no guarantee the challenge will be won. The chance of creating a shooting opportunity with a pass to feet was much higher.

Mentally, the work had begun too. Players were going out onto the pitch as equals, rather than the perhaps self-perceived better team. There were exceptions, naturally, though they were becoming fewer. While performances were frequently unspectacular, they were necessary to build the confidence again. The consecutive wins at the start of the season had felt a long time ago and the fans could be forgiven for feeling cynical – there was nothing to say this wouldn't be another one of those nearly moments for the club. How many times had they seen it before, as manager after manager had come in to solve the problems the previous one had failed to, but, in doing so, fallen foul of a completely new set of failures?

Speaking personally, it took me a long time to get to grips with Roberto Mancini. I had always been of the opinion that Mark Hughes deserved more time to get his side's good form to return, but what's happened at City since changing the boss has proved to me why the chairman did what he felt he had to. And while the change may have been badly handled, it was precisely what was needed: the fans may have taken time to warm to the Italian's methods, but there can be little in the way of an argument against the position that they have, on the whole, worked.

Throughout his first full season in charge, Roberto Mancini spoke

Burnley 1-6 Manchester City
Saturday 3 April 2010, Premier League

City: Given, Onuoha, Toure (c), Kompany, Sylvinho (de Jong 68), Barry, Vieira, A Johnson, Bellamy, Adebayor (Santa Cruz 80), Tevez (Nimely 83)
Goals: Adebayor (4, 45), Bellamy (5), Tevez (7), Vieira (20), Kompany (58)

As the end of the season approached, City went into their final run-in with form on their side. A 3-0 win over Wigan was followed by the Blues' first ever 6-1 demolition of their opposition in the Premier League. It came at Burnley and, just seven minutes into the match, it was all over, as Adebayor, Bellamy and Tevez had all already scored.

The score could have hit more than six had it not been for the horrendous rain that threatened to force referee Alan Wiley to abandon the game. Fortunately, he didn't and Roberto Mancini recorded the first of his 6-1 away wins with City.

constantly about the club needing to have a 'winning mentality'. It seems odd to say, but this is something that was needed from the top down. He was right – three and a half trophyless decades had reduced players, staff and fans to having the attitude that, as long as they gave a good account of themselves, they should be happy. Years of instability and turmoil had taken their toll. Manchester City was a mid-table club and that's where they belonged.

Except that just wasn't true.

And an attitude that is so easily destroyed is so difficult to build. Giving everybody inside the club the belief that they are winners isn't easy, when years of cynicism have shrouded the minds of the fans. They daren't believe it because it will bite them on the bottom, as it had done so many times in the past. They'll be duped. And they will once again become that laughing stock, simply because they had dared to let themselves dream that this was the time when everything changed for City.

Emmanuel Adebayor

Born: 26 Feb 1984
Signed: 19 Jul 2009
Sold: 12 Aug 2012

Apps: 36 (9 sub)
Goals: 19
Yellow Cards: 1
Red Cards: 1
Notes: Scored City's first ever European hat-trick in a win over Lech Poznan.

The love for the club had always remained, as had the hope that things would get better. But in our heart of hearts, we knew nothing would really change. City would fail in that way they always do and the world would laugh, while others would enjoy the silverware and the limelight for their quality of football. When someone's had their mental attitude battered to that level of belief, it's difficult to get them to believe otherwise.

Mancini did it the best way: on the pitch.

In winning games, confidence slowly returned. Perhaps what actually separates Roberto Mancini from many of those who have taken on the monumental job of managing Manchester City isn't as much to do with the transfer funds he's had at his disposal, but his ability to change the entire club's attitude and opinion of itself. The funds have helped, of course, however to put any success at City down to that sole factor is a misguided conclusion to reach: the very thought that a richly assembled team can compete without management, tactical instruction and a rigid training schedule is nothing short of naïve.

After all, Mark Hughes had been given a seemingly bottomless pit of money and the quality in the first half of that 2009-10 season was far below the second.

Maybe the biggest reason City have come on leaps and bounds under the Italian is his opinion of himself. As a player, he was always one of the most important for the team. And he took it upon himself to be the best player on the pitch: if he didn't constantly improve, he couldn't help the team improve. He had the ability that others didn't and he didn't want to waste it. In management, he's the same and thinks the same of his players.

Soft and cuddly on the outside, especially in front of television cameras, Mancini is a cold and ruthless man. There is very little sentiment in his decision-making. He separated himself from his personal feelings when making decisions that affected the club. If something wasn't the best, then it wasn't good enough for him. It wasn't good enough for Manchester City.

Previous managers simply tried to change the club's on-field fortunes. The appointment of Roberto Mancini was where that changed. He recognised how important it was to get the right people to believe in what the club were trying to achieve.

And, for a while, the Blues reaped the benefits.

Roberto Mancini's First Press Conference
Garry Cook begins by reading a prepared statement.

Garry Cook: "The intention, of course, was to tell Mark immediately after the game on Saturday. That would then give Roberto a full week to prepare for the game at the weekend. Regreattably – and I repeat, regrettably – against all of our efforts, the rumours of discussions with Roberto Mancini became public before the game.

"Once Mark was informed, I informed his staff. And then consequently, the players themselves were informed, which is why Kolo Toure and Shay Given were asked to attend a meeting post game. There is no player rebellion. And the playing and the training staff have been going about their business today as usual, most professionally, led by Roberto and Brian Kidd.

"The decision to end Mark's tenure was a unanimous decision by the owner, the chairman, myself and the board, as was the decision to appoint Roberto. Like any other business, we have plans, we have targets, but we also have to have contingencies. The contingencies are for when those plans and targets are not being met.

"The decision to seriously look at options managerially was taken just three weeks ago. This was following the Hull City game. But I think it's important to know – and I'd like to stress – that Roberto was only offered the job after the Spurs game. We negotiated on Thursday. We finalised an agreement on Friday. And he was **not** in the stadium on Saturday, as was falsely reported.

"With the points that we've made, I just want to say there is nothing more for me to add to this process. It's been a difficult three days and it's a process of change that we've all had to go through. You'll find everything we've said today in a statement. It will be reported on the website. And I repeat, there is really nothing further to add on this subject."

Journalist 1: "Why did you put him through that on Saturday, Garry? Why didn't you..."

Journalist 2: "Do you feel embarrassed?"

Journalist 1: "...why didn't you do it on Friday or Saturday morning?"

Press Officer: "Guys…"

Journalist 1: "Why did you make him stand in front of 47,000 people knowing that he was leaving?"

Garry Cook: "As again, I'd like to just add there is no further comment I'd like to make on this subject."

Journalist 2: "Do you not feel embarrassed?"

Later, Roberto Mancini is asked about his appointment.

Journalist 3: "So when were you first contacted by Manchester City?"

Roberto Mancini: "They called me the day after Tottenham."

Journalist 3: "So no time before the Tottenham game?"

Roberto Mancini: "Two weeks ago, I meet Khaldoon, but the first time… but they call after the day Tottenham Hotspur. Not before."

Journalist 3: "How difficult has this situation been for you, bearing in mind you're talking about a job where a manager is already in that job?"

Roberto Mancini: "I don't know this, but my job is a manager. I stayed in Inter Milan for four years and I won seven trophies in four years. And at the end of the season, they sacked me. This is our job. You stay in a club for many years – sometimes two years, three years, it depends. I don't know. I don't want to look back because I stay here to train."

Journalist 4: "Have you been set a target to achieve?"

Roberto Mancini: "My squad usually play to win, always. I think…"

Journalist 4: "Mark Hughes was set sixth and then 70 points. Have you been set… Is this your target?"

Roberto Mancini: "My target if possible is to arrive in the top four. But it's my objective. My target. I think this is possible."

Journalist 5: "Do you expect to be fired if you don't make the top four?"

Roberto Mancini: "No. I think and I hope to stay here for many, many years."

Chapter Four
A Winning Mentality

MY GRAN ONCE PROPHETICALLY ANNOUNCED that getting back behind the wheel of a car was difficult when you'd had a long time away from driving. I've tidied that up a fair bit, because it was probably 30 to 40 seconds of ramblings about how it wasn't easy to judge the size of your car or how it felt cumbersome or unnatural to be driving again, but you get the idea. Her point was that, when you're out of practice, something becomes tricky once again.

Naturally, the more out of practice a person is, the more difficult the task at hand is to complete. My gran had needed a new hip and had spent 18 months unable to use her right leg and therefore unable to pop down to the shops or have a ride out to my uncle's house. Manchester City, on the other hand, had gone 35 years without adding to their trophy collection.

If an 18-month hiatus is difficult, a 35-year break is likely to be damn near impossible.

When Joe Royle was managing City in the Premier League back in the 2000-01 season, the Blues started brightly. In the first ten games, the club won four and drew two (and those four victories would turn out to be half of all the matches they took maximum points from that campaign). Ok, so maybe there was no tearing up of trees, but it was looking good for survival: less than a third of the way through the season and more than a third of the way to that hallowed 40 points mark.

Joe Royle
18 Feb 1998 – 21 May 2001

PL Played: 38
PL Won: 8
PL Drawn: 10
PL Lost: 20

PL Goals For: 41
PL Goals Against: 65

PL Win Rate: 21.05%

But then November happened. It was the worst run of form for the club that season, as they went on to lose six matches in a row. A 5-0 drubbing of Everton at Maine Road stalled the slide, but that one solitary victory would become a statistic of one win in 17 games (six others being draws and the remaining ten being defeats).

During that time, the manager commented that City were in the habit of not winning. And, while there's only so far that argument can go, it does hold a little bit of water. A rich vein of form leads teams to continue to play well and turn in good performances as confidence runs through the squad, so equally the reverse must be true; as poor performances rack up, players are already on a psychological down before kick-off.

Now, we can argue all day about the value of the supernatural when it comes to the influence of football matches – do superstitions really work, for example? – but a mind that is convinced the worst will happen will be one that, when leading and on top of a match, will become conservative and try to protect what it has. Cue the inevitable mistake under pressure and the equaliser. A mind that is flying high with confidence will see that spell of

Manchester City 5-0 Everton
Saturday 9 December 2000, Premier League

City: Weaver, Charvet, Tiatto, Howey, Dunne, Haaland (c) (Wiekens 46), Whitley, Horlock, Wright-Phillips (Kennedy 61), Wanchope, Goater (Dickov 43)
Goals: Wanchope (10), Howey (22), Goater (41), Dickov (53), Naysmith (og 65)

When the City fans rocked up at Maine Road on a rainy Saturday afternoon, very few will have been expecting an early Christmas present from the team. A run of six straight defeats was brought to an end in stunning style, as Joe Royle's City smashed five past one of his old clubs. After the game, the manager said it "had been coming for some time" and "someone was going to get that", believing his side had put in better performances than the results showed.

In truth, it did little to boost City's form and they wouldn't win again until the end of February, picking up six points from a possible 30 in that time. After the Everton game, the Blues were five points ahead of the relegation zone. After their next win, they were one point inside it. The club's fight was admirable, but this was a team very similar to the one that just escaped Division Two and there was only so much they could do to avoid the drop.

domination as a chance to kill off the tie. This probably goes some way to explain why clubs can dish out a battering in one fixture at the start of a season, but succumb to a feeble defeat in the reverse game.

So, you can see where Royle was coming from: losing and drawing was becoming the norm and was a habit that needed breaking. Of course, the history books show that that never happened and City slipped out of the league with a defeat at Ipswich, a year to the day after they had been promoted at Blackburn.

Expand that thought further and a club that has become

used to being knocked out in the early rounds of cup competitions is one that doesn't expect to reach the final. It's one that's happy to give a good account of themselves, get through a few stages to boost revenue, but not be too disappointed with elimination to a club that's higher up the league table.

FA Cup Record 1999-2010

1999: Wimbledon (a), *R3*, 1-0
2000: Leeds (h), *R4*, 2-5
2001: Liverpool (a), *R5*, 4-2
2002: Newcastle (a), *R5*, 1-0
2003: Liverpool (h), *R3*, 0-1
2004: Man Utd (a), *R5*, 4-2
2005: Oldham (a), *R3*, 1-0
2006: West Ham (h), *R6*, 1-2
2007: Blackburn (a), *R6*, 2-0
2008: Sheff Utd (a), *R4*, 2-1
2009: Nottm Forest (h), *R3*, 0-3
2010: Stoke (a), *R5*, 3-1

You could probably forgive City for giving a poor showing in the domestic cups when they were on their tour of the lower leagues, especially as, in one season, dropping to the third tier of English football meant entering the FA Cup in the first round and not the third.

Having won the League Cup in 1976 with an overhead kick from Dennis Tueart, the Blues began to falter somewhat in the trophy market. In fact, there was a Division One title in 2001 as Kevin Keegan's City waltzed away and blitzed the league with some outstanding football... and that was it. The Blues visited the FA Cup final in 1981, but were beaten by Tottenham in a replay.

They were quickly becoming a club that was getting used to losing and making a habit of making their excuses and leaving the cups.

And, although players, managers, chairmen, and even stadiums change, that pressure still builds. It's a collective for the club; musings in the press and discussion from fans makes it obvious to anybody in the team that the lack of silverware has been ongoing for however many years. However many decades. And that, in turn, creates a

Tottenham Hotspur 3-2 Manchester City
Thursday 14 May 1981, FA Cup Final (replay)

City: Corrigan, Ranson, McDonald (Tueart 79), Reid, Power (c), Caton, Bennett, Gow, MacKenzie, Hutchison, Reeves
Goals: MacKenzie (11), Reeves (pen 50)

City fans returning to Wembley on the Thursday after their last visit five days earlier will have been cursing their luck before kick off. Having taken the lead against Tottenham in the final through Tommy Hutchison, the Blues then conceded an equaliser as a poor free kick from Glenn Hoddle cruelly deflected off City's goalscorer and beat Joe Corrigan.

And after going behind in the early stages of the replay, the Blues hit back almost immediately. Kevin Reeves put City in the lead, before Garth Crooks pulled Spurs level. It was then down to Ricky Villa to break the fans' hearts, as he scored the goal that went down in history as one of the best to grace a final.

In the eyes of City fans, though, that should have been Steve MacKenzie's brilliant volley from the edge of the box.

pressure that builds more as the years tick by.

That was the task facing Roberto Mancini at the beginning of his first full season in charge. It wasn't just about being successful to make sure he was doing a good job, to keep himself in the managerial role, or to achieve his aims personally or professionally. For him to do any of that, it was all about breaking the viscious circle.

The weight of 35 years of pressure is heavy upon the shoulders of the club and its players. As the team progresses through each round of the cup, the draws become more difficult and that pressure increases again. Mancini's job was to ease it and build a squad with the mentality that was strong enough to cope with it.

Mancini's first crack at a cup actually came in the first few weeks of his tenure as manager. Mark Hughes had guided the Blues to the semi final of the League Cup in 2009 and, in the January of the next year, the club had been drawn against rivals Manchester United. And, collectively, the fans sighed.

When the first leg of that tie came around, the feeling of tension around Eastlands was awful and hard to bear. This was the first semi final the club had been involved in since I had been born and my then 22-year-old self was very uncomfortable watching the match. In my mind, City would fail: it's what they did. I'd grown up with nothing

League Cup Record 1999-2010
98-99: Derby, *R2*, 1-1 (a), 0-1 (h)
99-00: Soton, *R2*, 0-0 (h), 4-3 (a)
00-01: Ipswich (h), *R5*, 1-2
01-02: Blackburn (a), *R4*, 2-0
02-03: Wigan (a), *R3*, 1-0
03-04: Tottenham (a), *R4*, 3-1
04-05: Arsenal (h), *R3*, 1-2
05-06: Doncaster (a), *R2*, 1-1 (pens)
06-07: Chesterfield (a), *R2*, 2-1
07-08: Tottenham (h), *R5*, 0-2
08-09: Brighton (a), *R2*, 2-2 (pens)
09-10: Man Utd, *R6*, 2-1 (h), 3-1 (a)

other than my beloved football club building up my hopes only to let me down, so what would make that year any more special? That feeling was fully vindicated when Ryan Giggs opened the scoring, not only putting more pressure on City and pegging them back, but adding an away goal to the mix.

However, one dubious penalty and a close-range header later, and City were leading after the first leg (thanks in no small part also to a clearance off the line by Nedum Onuoha, when a Michael Owen shot had wrong-footed Shay Given). Leaving the stadium, the fans were relieved at having the lead, but equally there still a deep nervous feeling about the return leg.

Those fears turned out to be correctly held, as City provided a master class in building you up to let you down.

At Old Trafford, it was goalless at half time. If the Blues could hold on, they would be into their first final since the early 80s. Cue two quick goals from the Reds and cue the inevitable sinking feeling that came with it. A Tevez back-heel flick pulled a goal back and levelled the tie on aggregate, allowing the fans to dream once more, though it would now take extra time and penalties if City weren't to score another.

But just as thoughts were turning to the extra period, Wayne Rooney nicked it with just a couple of minutes to play, unmarked inside the six-yard box. The pressure had taken its toll again. While the fans had hoped it would end in a positive, it could be said there were few who were totally surprised that it didn't.

Actually getting the trophy-winning monkey off the club's back and changing the mentality of the players weren't the only tasks Roberto Mancini had to face up to. On top of all of that, getting the fans to actually believe would be even harder. Expecting to get let down has exactly the same effect as expecting to lose a game: the fans get tense, that tension transfers to the players and mistakes are made. The fans are an important part to getting results, too.

Patrick Vieira

Born: 23 Jun 1976
Signed: 8 Jan 2010
Retired: 31 May 2011

Apps: 25 (21 sub)
Goals: 6
Yellow Cards: 6
Red Cards: 0
Notes: Won his fifth FA Cup with City in 2011, scoring three in the run.

Just over two weeks before City lost to United in the League Cup semi final second leg, Mancini added a veteran midfielder to the Blues' squad in Patrick Vieira. The Frenchman had worked with the manager previously at Inter Milan and, when asked why he had signed a player who was clearly on the downward arc of his career given his age, Mancini talked about Vieira's mentality. He called him a winner.

At the time, it would have been very easy to dismiss this as hyperbole. There was the feeling among the fans that Vieira was simply a half-season signing to add some experience to the midfield and to act as a mentor to the younger players at the club – but, at the end of the campaign when the World Cup winner signed a year extension, it became clear that Mancini was very serious. What better way to make sure a squad is capable of lifting silverware than by building it around someone who's won everything?

This was part one of the plan: getting the players comfortable dealing with the pressures of three decades of expectations. In Vieira, he had a cool head and a man who was strong mentally, with enough influence for that to rub off on others in the squad. A man who was reliable at the end of matches to make sure a win didn't become a draw and a draw didn't become a defeat.

The fans would be a more difficult nut to crack; the only way they would be convinced that things were changing would be to actually improve fortunes on the pitch, and the club's form in the Premier League at the start of 2010-11, in no small part, did that. There was a blip in the autumn, which saw defeats to Wolves and Arsenal, with home goalless draws against Birmingham and Manchester United thrown in for good measure, but, on the whole, the fans were being treated to much better spells of football than ever before.

There was a growing confidence towards the end of games that the Blues could see a result out. It may have been the Manchester derby remembered for absolutely nothing happening, but that 0-0 draw did a lot more towards the fans' mentality than a lot of onlookers thought: in three of the four games with United the season before, City had lost to a goal in stoppage time. This season, and when coming under pressure, the defence held firm and looked like they could play on all night and not concede.

True, they never looked like scoring, either, but that was a step up on losing in the last minute.

The very fact that, as the Blues travelled to Craven Cottage and bagged four, the fans had enough confidence to mock critics in the press who had branded the club's style of play boring spoke volumes. City were becoming a possession team, able to string 30 or 40 passes together to try and work an opening. It was good to watch for the fans, but many outsiders mistook it for City killing the game and stopping the opposition from scoring. It was "boring, boring City" indeed.

With the mental barriers being torn down as the months progressed, Roberto Mancini embarked on his second FA Cup campaign. His first – in 2010 – had seen the Blues

Fulham 1-4 Manchester City
Sunday 21 November 2010
Premier League

City: Hart, Zabaleta, K Toure, Kompany, Kolarov, de Jong, Y Toure, Barry (Vieira 82), Silva (Milner 88), Tevez (c) (A Johnson 77), Jo
Goals: Tevez (6, 55), Zabaleta (32), Y Toure (34)

Under pressure, Roberto Mancini took his side to Craven Cottage and sent a message to the footballing world. Up to this point, there were questions as to whether Mancini was doing anything to move City in the right direction, but afterwards the fans were convinced, even if some of the watching world remained less so. This was a turning point for the club, coming out of their winless streak in style.

After this game, the Blues moved into the top four of the Premier League and never dropped out for the rest of the season. The fans witnessed some of the best passing football the team had produced in years.

succumb to Stoke in extra time a replay at the Britannia Stadium, following a red card for Emmanuel Adebayor.

The 2010-11 season saw Mancini's first crack at the competition since instilling a new found confidence into the club.

Chapter Five
We Will Find A Brighter Day

A T THE BEGINNING OF THE 2010-11 season, following several high profile signings and the newfound defensive sturdiness, Roberto Mancini's Manchester City had made an impression on me. I had, like a lot of fans, fully expected that his stewardship would have ended in the summer of 2010, believing he was simply a stopgap replacement for Mark Hughes until another was available. But, as the teams walked out at White Hart Lane and the Italian took the away dugout, I was willing to give him a chance. It would be fair to say I was still feeling underwhelmed by his appointment at that time, but, equally, I wasn't willing to write him off.

The first question of the day was whether Shay Given would be starting in goal or whether the place at the top of the team sheet would go to Joe Hart, following a brilliant season on loan at Birmingham. Within roughly 20 first half minutes, Mancini's decision to go with youth over experience was fully justified, as three save of the season contenders had kept the scores level.

After the rivalry that City had had with Spurs the season before and given the performance of the home side, it was a relief to hear the final whistle when the score remained goalless. And, in truth, City didn't draw the game 0-0, they won it 0-0: Spurs had enough chances to win three or four matches, but were denied time and again thanks to the brilliance of the visiting defence.

That set the precedent for the season.

It wasn't all smelling of roses, however. As the autumn turned to winter, there were murmurings in the press that all wasn't well in Mancini's camp and, to go along with it, there were some dissenting voices from the fans. At the back end of October and the start of November, the club went on a run of one win in five games and critics were beginning to wonder if a victory at West Brom, sandwiched in between defeats against Arsenal, Wolves and Lech Poznan and successive home goalless draws against Manchester United and Birmingham were signs that something was going wrong. Maybe the club would end up on a slide like the seven successive draws the year before.

A 4-1 demolition of Fulham at Craven Cottage followed and it sent the Blues back into the top four in the Premier League. After that match – on Sunday 21 November – the club never moved out of the Champions League positions for the rest of the season. City definitely felt like they were moving in the right direction, albeit at times with the handbrake left on. Still,

Sunday 24 October 2010
Man City 0-3 Arsenal (PL)

Saturday 30 October 2010
Wolves 2-1 Man City (PL)

Thursday 4 November 2010
Lech Poznan 3-1 Man City (EL)

Sunday 7 November 2010
West Brom 0-2 Man City (PL)

Wednesday 10 November 2010
Man City 0-0 Man Utd (PL)

Saturday 13 November 2010
Man City 0-0 Birmingham (PL)

that was better than handbrake off and rolling backwards down a steep hill towards a river, as had been the case at the club for some time.

At the end of that month, Noel Gallagher of Oasis fame and Serge Pizzorno from Kasabian got together in London to pull some small black balls out of a plastic container. Serge had managed to grab his beloved Leicester City a home tie. And, rather predictably, Noel had decided that the team he supported, Manchester City, would be the visitors.

On Sunday 9 January 2011, the two clubs met at the Walkers Stadium. It was to be a day of reunions and the perfect tie to start that year's FA Cup run: former City manager Sven Goran Eriksson was reunited with his old club. Roberto Mancini was brought back to face his old mentor, after a spell as Sven's assistant manager at Lazio. And it seemed a poignant draw, too, as news had broken in late 2010 that the ex-City striker Neil Young had been diagnosed with terminal cancer.

Young had scored the winning goal for City the last time they had won the FA Cup in 1969, in a final against Leicester. The supporters dedicated the tie to him, wearing red and black because they were colours the club had worn in that final. Roberto Mancini donned a red and black scarf on top of his now trademark blue and white one. During the 24th minute, fans performed a Poznan, turning their backs to the play and jumping up and down in unison, to mark the minute Young scored the winning goal. It was one of the first Poznans the supporters performed.

In all of this, the fact the game finished all square is bizarrely one of the forgotten details of the day. Sol Bamba had given the hosts the lead from their first attack of the game in the very first minute. I'm sure there have been worse starts to FA Cup campaigns down the years, but I certainly can't remember them. Indeed, a free header from the centre-back was all the encouragement he needed to nod home from a corner.

Just over 20 minutes later, James Milner levelled the count. Scoring his first goal for the club had perhaps taken longer than expected, but it was certainly not one anybody would have turned down at the time, as the Championship side was looking for a notable Premier League scalp. Following that left-footed equaliser, City took the lead just moments before half time, thanks to a cheeky Carlos Tevez back-heel flick.

James Milner

Born: 4 Jan 1986
Signed: 18 Aug 2010
Sold: -

Apps: 78 (36 sub)
Goals: 8
Yellow Cards: 11
Red Cards: 1
Notes: Opened the scoring in City's victorious 2011 FA Cup campaign.

Second half pressure inevitably followed and City's defence were tested to the full. As it looked like this newfound resilience would hold out, Joe Hart pulled out an uncharacteristic mistake, dropping the ball at the feet of Andy King and presenting him with an open goal. He decided it was too good an opportunity to turn down and smeared the goalkeeper's face with egg, before slotting into the empty net.

A replay beckoned.

Sven's return to Eastlands wasn't as pleasant for him as some of the times he'd had at the club, however. A brilliant solo goal from Carlos Tevez gave the home side the lead, before a penalty equaliser from Paul Gallagher pulled Leicester level. But two goals in two minutes, one from Patrick Vieira and the other from Adam Johnson, virtually killed off the tie.

With eight minutes of regulation time to play, though, referee Mark Halsey decided that the game needed livening up. Some officials do this with a dubious red card. Others,

Referee: Mark Halsey

Premier League Record
W7 D2 L14 F30 A36
Win Rate: 30.43%

Yellow Cards
For City: 17
For Opponents: 18

Red Cards
For City: 1
For Opponents: 1

Penalties
For City: 3
For Opposition: 2

as happened in this replay, take the much bolder and more daring move of assisting a goal for the losing side – a loose ball in the midfield caught the referee and completely deceived the City defence. Lloyd Dyer raced clear and pulled another goal back, before Aleksandar Kolarov did what he does best: belted one in from the edge of the area because 'it'll look amazing if this one goes in'. And went in it did.

For the record, I don't think Halsey *intentionally* assisted Leicester's second goal and I don't think any referees 'even things out a bit'.

And so, after beating Sven's club, Sven's former club would travel to another of Sven's former clubs in Notts County. Still following this? Good, because I had to re-read that last bit about five times to make sure it made sense and even now I'm sort of just hoping it's right.

Meadow Lane was the destination for City's fourth round tie. It was another game that would end up being filed away safely in the 'not a classic' folder, probably not helped that the pitch resembled a freshly ploughed field that had just hosted a demolition derby in the rain.

Therefore, what was originally a banana skin tie had become a banana skin covered in cooking oil tie – even slippier and a hazard zone that covered a much larger area. It was little surprise when Neal Bishop opened the scoring for the home side. Given how long the Blues had gone without adding to their trophy cabinet – asbestos removal workers needed less protective clothing than anybody wishing to get the dust off and open the trophy cabinet at City – if they were going to end the drought, they were determined to do it the hard way.

Edin Dzeko

Born: 17 Mar 1986
Signed: 7 Jan 2011
Sold: -

Apps: 62 (47 sub)
Goals: 40
Yellow Cards: 10
Red Cards: 0
Notes: Kept City in the FA Cup at Notts County in 2011 and scored the equaliser in the title winning game against QPR in May 2012.

With just over ten minutes of the game left to play, Edin Dzeko announced himself to City fans as a man capable of scoring important goals. The late equaliser in this match was his first for the club, as a low cross into the box left him with a virtual open goal. With the surface being as predictable as a Mario Balotelli house party, Dzeko's effort could well have landed in the centre of Nottingham rather than the back of the onion bag – the big striker did well to divert it into the roof of the net. It doesn't matter how they go in, after all.

It was this game that really revived Micah Richards' career with City, too. Before this match, I had spent months losing patience with the defender, believing that he'd not shown anything near his best form since Sven had moved him to centre-back to partner Richard Dunne about three years earlier. Yet, back at right-back, Mancini had seemingly breathed a whole new life into him and the bombing runs down the flank that have become his trademark at City began in this very tie. It was one of his first that provided the assist for Dzeko.

So, it was another unwanted replay in a fixture list that was becoming more congested than my left nostril whenever the temperature peaks higher than 'tepid'. And let me tell you, as soon as the calendar flicks to April, I can't breathe using my nose until it's October.

Nevertheless, the Blues made light work of their opponents when back at the City of Manchester Stadium. Okay, so there was a slight scare, as Notts County did strike the frame of Hart's goal, but Patrick Vieira popped up to put the home side in the lead shortly after. Then, as the legs from the visitors began to tire, City ran riot: Vieira added another, before Dzeko fed Tevez and Tevez fed Dzeko. The scoring was rounded off by Micah Richards, as he swivelled and volleyed in the area with an effort that shocked even him when it found the back of the net.

Banana skin safely navigated then, and City faced Premier League opponents for the first time on their run. They had known before kick-off in their replay who they'd been drawn against and it was safe to say the fans were confident knowing that previous games against Aston Villa, especially at home, usually resulted in victory.

Home Record Against Aston Villa

10-11: 4-0 win (PL)
09-10: 3-1 win (PL)
08-09: 2-0 win (PL)
07-08: 1-0 win (PL)
06-07: 0-2 loss (PL)
05-06: 2-1 win (FAC)
05-06: 3-1 win (PL)
04-05: 2-0 win (PL)
03-04: 4-1 win (PL)
02-03: 3-1 win (PL)

Half an eye had already been cast to the sixth round by the time kick off came. Due to City's fixture congestion they, once again, knew their opponents – the draw on Sunday 20 February 2011 took place before City had had the chance to take on the Midlands club and the same had happened to

Home Record
Against Everton

10-11: 1-2 loss (PL)
09-10: 0-2 loss (PL)
08-09: 0-1 loss (PL)
07-08: 0-2 loss (PL)
06-07: 2-1 win (PL)
05-06: 2-0 win (PL)
04-05: 0-1 loss (PL)
03-04: 5-1 win (PL)
02-03: 3-1 win (PL)

the eventual opponents, Premier League Everton or Championship Reading. It was generally assumed among City fans that it would be Everton who made it through and against the Toffees where the cup run would come to an end.

But, the day before the Blues took on Villa, fans watched in astonishment as the underdogs went to Goodison Park and won, thanks to a first half goal from one time Manchester City defender Matt Mills. The Footballing Gods were smiling down on the club for what felt like the first time in a long time (if you believe in reincarnation, then clearly someone at City had done something so horrendous in a past life that they were still being punished for it). For the winner of the fifth round tie, a home game against lower league opposition awaited.

As a club, I've never particularly liked Aston Villa. It's got nothing to do with anything objective, but more that I don't like the colour of the kit they play in. Same for West Ham and Burnley, since you asked. However, I felt for their fans that evening, as they watched a heavily rotated and understrength team get well and truly outplayed by a full strength City side: "Let's pretend we scored a goal" echoed from the away end, followed by a loud cheer. I suddenly remembered back to the days of watching City and having to make my own fun, too. Not nice.

It took just five minutes for the net to bulge and, if it's at all possible so quickly into the match, it had been coming. Yaya Toure slammed the ball home from close range, following some pinball from a corner. Mario Balotelli added a goal of the season contender before half time – a side footed half volley that bounced over his shoulder – and the match was rounded off in style with a clinical finish from David Silva.

Continuing the tradition of knowing the opposition should City win the coming game, City knew who they'd face in the semi final should they beat Reading, playing as they were in the evening of the day the draw was made. Manchester United waited at Wembley for the winner. Suddenly, thoughts of winning the cup had become anxiety about a potential Manchester derby semi final. United had knocked the City out in the League Cup semi final the season before, and if they did it again this year it'd be hard to take, especially at Wembley.

A late header from the in-form Micah Richards header was enough for City to progress,

Liverpool 3-0 Manchester City
Monday 11 April 2011
Premier League

City: Hart, Boyata, Kompany, Lescott, Kolarov, Barry, Y Toure, Milner (Silva 59), A Johnson, Tevez (c) (Balotelli 13 (de Jong 83)), Dzeko
Goals: -

Bad news before the FA Cup semi final seemed to follow City around like a bad smell. Seconds before Andy Carroll opened the scoring in this match, City's talisman for the season, Carlos Tevez, pulled up holding his hamstring. Seconds after the goal, he was substituted.

More bad defending resulted in a second goal for the home side and, a mere minute after the visitors had kicked off again, Liverpool won the ball back and scored their third. It was a miracle it finished 3-0, based on City's performance.

It was as if the Footballing Gods were conspiring against the club ahead of their most important game of the season so far.

just as it looked like it might have taken a replay to separate the sides. Reading were a tough nut to crack: despite the home team's domination, the chances were rarely clear cut. It wasn't especially the most encouraging performance to lead into a Manchester derby.

Worse, on the Monday evening before the semi final, City lost their leading scorer to injury. Carlos Tevez limped out of the embarrassing 3-0 defeat at Anfield, as Liverpool ran riot. Fortunately, Wayne Rooney had found himself suspended for the trip to Wembley – thanks to comments made to a camera during a game live on Sky Sports. It became a question of who would cope best without their top man for the season. Many were worried it'd be the Reds, but that's three decades of built-up cynicism for you.

Confession time: I, David James Mooney, wasn't at Wembley for that semi final match. Mind you, my nerves probably would never have taken it if I were. I was, in fact, in the United States, having planned a holiday that weekend for three reasons: it was cheap; City are never normally in the FA Cup semi final, so it seemed fairly safe to go; if City weren't in the semi final, it was Tottenham at home – and that's always a banker for the North London club, right?

So I missed the pre-match Poznan. I missed the point-blank save by Hart from Berbatov. I missed the Barry effort that hit the side netting. I missed Scholes leaving some stud marks on Zabaleta's thigh. And, most of all, I missed Yaya Toure nicking the ball off Michael Carrick and sliding it through Edwin van der Sar's legs.

I saw it all on television, of course (well, the second half anyway; I was stuck on the freeway for the first half), but that's not the same.

And with Stoke tonking Bolton in the other semi, it left just two teams in the competition and Manchester City had suddenly become the favourites. Being City fans, though, the supporters in the stands weren't taking anything for granted: Stoke had been a thorn in City's side away from Eastlands for some time and, if there were ever a football club that could do all the hard work and mess up the easy

Manchester City 1-0 Stoke City
Saturday 14 May 2011, FA Cup Final

City: Hart, Richards, Kompany, Lescott, Kolarov, Barry (A Johnson 73), de Jong, Y Toure, Silva (Vieira 90), Balotelli, Tevez (c) (Zabaleta 89)
Goals: Y Toure (74)

Having endured 35 years without seeing their team win a trophy, the City fans piled into Wembley filled with hope and expectation. And trepidation, because, let's face it, the hardest part had been done and they were going into the game as the team expected to win. If history's taught us anything it's that when City are expected to win, they make a big deal out of winning.

The Blues created the better chances, but struggled to find the net. It was an edgy match, as both teams didn't over-commit for fear of losing it. Eventually, it was City that gambled well into the second half and, just as the Stoke bench had commented on ITV that they were doing well and were hoping to keep stifling City, the very next move resulted in the game's only goal. Yaya Toure wellied it into the net from close range, after some pinball in the six-yard box left him with a ball that sat up nicely.

Relief filled the City end, as the referee blew for full time. Roberto Mancini celebrated like one of the fans, as he fulfilled his promise of tearing down the banner showing the years since the club's last trophy from Old Trafford. Their own was then unfurled on the pitch: 00 Years.

stuff, it was the Blues.

They needn't have worried. After a few hairy moments – including one cracking save from Joe Hart, one-on-one with Kenwyne Jones – it was City who took the lead; Yaya Toure again, this time finishing from a loose ball in the box, following some good work from Balotelli and Silva. Same player and the same end as in the semi final – though just a bit later in the match.

After some pressure towards the end of the game, in which Stoke didn't actually threaten City's goal, but did have a series of corners to test the Blues' defensive capabilities, the final whistle blew and City had their first piece of silverware in 35 years.

In the space of a season and a half, Roberto Mancini had turned a squad of nearly men into one of winners. The fans had followed suit, too; full of confidence about what the future would hold.

Yaya Toure

Born: 13 May 1983
Signed: 2 Jul 2010
Sold: -

Apps: 132 (2 sub)
Goals: 28
Yellow Cards: 28
Red Cards: 0
Notes: Scored in his first two trips to Wembley with City, both of them 1-0 wins.

Chapter Six
A Season Too Soon

AS THE SUMMER OF 2011 came to a close, a lot of my fellow City fans were talking about a title challenge. Not me. Instead, I was again considering that 2011-12 would be "a season too soon" for a title challenge. In truth, part of me was worried that I'd say it was on and then it would collapse in front of my eyes, while another part of me was a little scared about what it would bring to the club. City had never managed a title challenge in my lifetime, not in the top division anyway. It didn't make any sense to think it might happen, despite there being evidence of change from the years previously.

In fact, when asked for my prediction on *Blue Moon Live*, I plumped for second position in the league come May, commenting again that it was probably "a year too soon". I feel slightly foolish now, but I have to admit that until City did win the league, every year would have probably been "a year too soon". Winning the FA Cup is very different: favourable draws and lucky bounces can play a whole lot more of a part, given there's just six ties to win from round three to the final. The league, though, is a long 38-game slog over nine months, where long-term injuries, suspensions,

10-11: 3rd (71 points)
09-10: 5th (67 points)
08-09: 10th (50 points)
07-08: 9th (55 points)
06-07: 14th (42 points)
05-06: 15th (43 points)
04-05: 8th (52 points)
03-04: 16th (41 points)
02-03: 9th (51 points)

and losses of form have a much more damaging effect.

Plus it's not all about the team. It may sound bizarre to say, but the performances of other clubs are crucial. Take Swansea, for example – City battered them on the opening day of the season, but created few chances in the return fixture months later, as Swansea's fortunes had taken a turn for the better and City were under increasing pressure, duly falling to a disappointing defeat. Equally, there are times when rivals for a league position drop points and kick off earlier, meaning the pressure is lifted somewhat.

The challenge of winning the league was significantly harder than the year before. And that scared me.

When the teams ran out for the first pre-season friendly against Club America, just one new player had joined the ranks and was in the squad for the summer's warm-up games. Gael Clichy didn't appear to be the most high-profile signing the Blues would make, but he was the first arrival that would have a huge effect to strengthening the team. Aleksandar Kolarov – a left back, with a very adventurous attacking side to his game – had been exposed defensively on numerous occasions the year before and, while City fans hadn't really paid attention to Clichy at Arsenal, Roberto Mancini clearly had.

If there were to be any indication that the 2011-12 season was going to be eventful, it was after just 31 minutes of the pre-season match with LA Galaxy. Through on goal and with Edin Dzeko square, Mario Balotelli drew the ire of his manager by attempting a back-heeled finish, turning his back to the goalkeeper and trying to roll the ball home. He missed and Mancini, fuming at the level of disrespect for the opponents, pulled the Italian from the pitch straight away, swapping him for James Milner.

By the time the Blues jetted off to Ireland for the Dublin Super Cup, they had confirmed the signing of a man who was perhaps one of the most exciting players of his generation: The Argentine international and son-in-law of Diego Maradonna, Sergio Aguero. Having been away playing in the Copa America, Roberto Mancini decided that the Argentine wasn't fit enough to feature in any of the competition in Ireland, as a City reserve side (plus Adam Johnson) went on to beat an Irish XI by three goals to nil.

On the final day of July, City lifted the Dublin Super Cup – not the most prestigious trophy it has to be said and not the one the club would have been hoping for come the end of the season – with another 3-0 victory, this time over Roberto Mancini's former club Inter Milan. It was a much stronger team that played that match, and one that gave some sort of indication as to what plans the manager had for the campaign ahead.

The Community Shield seven days later was perhaps another perfect metaphor for how the season would pan out. It pitted City as FA Cup winners against United as Premier League winners. While the Blues barely got out of first gear, they did make a flying start and were leading by two goals to nil at half time. Though United

---

Mario Balotelli

Born: 12 Aug 1990
Signed: 13 Aug 2010
Sold: 31 Jan 2013

Apps: 49 (31 sub)
Goals: 30
Yellow Cards: 25
Red Cards: 4
Notes: Made only one assist in the league in 2011-12 – to Aguero against QPR.

Roberto Mancini vs. Manchester United

P12 W5 D1 L6 F20 A18

came back strongly and the Reds won it in the 94th minute.

Ok, so not a perfect metaphor, but you get the idea.

Sergio Aguero didn't feature in that game either, again deemed only fit enough for the bench but not fit enough to play any part – with the performance of the team and the fact the Argentine didn't get the opportunity to show what he could do, you could be forgiven for thinking Mancini didn't really mind losing the Community Shield. No, his thoughts were on the Premier League.

The Blues' first league match of the campaign was a Monday night tie against newly promoted Swansea. The fans were confident of a big win, but there was always the nagging doubt that there could be a surprise, as the plucky underdogs had nothing to lose in their first foray into the top flight since the early 80s. Following such a laboured performance in the season's curtain raiser, that worry wasn't going away, especially with the half time score standing at 0-0.

But, soon enough, the Manchester City Juggernaut had set off and Swansea were batted away by four goals. Edin Dzeko opened the scoring, before Sergio Aguero introduced himself to the Premier League. And, let's be honest, given what he did in his first season in England, it was never going to be a quiet introduction. Aguero tapped in City's second, assisted the third with an audacious lob over the goalkeeper before just keeping it in play and finding David Silva, and rounded things off by smashing one in from range in added time.

Welcome to Manchester, Sergio.

Given that the Blues went on to win the league on goal difference, this start to the season was important for the club. Over the first few games – where City beat Swansea (4-0), Bolton (3-2), and Tottenham (5-1) – it was actually United who were leading at the top of the table on goal difference.

Tottenham Hotspur 1-5 Manchester City
Sunday 28 August 2011, Premier League

City: Hart, Zabaleta (Richards 64), Lescott, Kompany (c), Clichy, Nasri, Barry, Silva, Y Toure, Aguero (Savic 75), Dzeko
Goals: Dzeko (35, 41, 55, 90+2), Aguero (60)

The old foe, Tottenham Hotspur, was City's first real test of the 2011-12 season. Traditionally a tough fixture for the club, City fans were looking at this game as the only problematic match of the opening couple of months. It was Spurs who had denied City a place in the Champions League two seasons earlier. The campaign before, the Blues scored just once – through a Peter Crouch own goal. So travelling to White Hart Lane was a difficult task.

After starting on the back-foot, the visitors eased into control of the game. A well-worked move put the opening goal on a plate for Dzeko. He doubled the lead with a brilliant header and, early in the second half, bagged his and City's third with a tap-in.

Aguero added his name to the scorers list, before the hosts grabbed a consolation and Dzeko got his fourth – the first time a City player bagged four in the league since David White did it against Aston Villa in 1991.

Test passed with flying colours.

That was largely down to a huge home win over Arsenal (8-2) and another large victory at the Reebok Stadium (5-0). But when United's victories became ones they had ground out by one goal (from the end of October to the start of December, four of United's five matches finished 1-0 and they didn't score more than one in a game from their 1-1 draw at Anfield on 15 October until they beat Wolves 4-1 at Old Trafford on 10 December – a run of seven games), City continued to blitz the opposition – the Blues scored at least two goals in every league game until they drew 1-1 at Liverpool in late November.

In fact, while we're getting statistical, by the time City first lost in the league when they visited Stamford Bridge in December, the Blues had racked up 48 goals. By that same round of matches, United had 35 (eight of which had come in that one aberration against Arsenal).

City's strikers were having a whale of a time in front of goal. Sergio Aguero was showing why he demanded such a high price, while Mario Balotelli seemingly scored whenever he started a game. Carlos Tevez had gone AWOL, following the now infamous incident in Munich, but the Blues didn't appear to be missing him. And, at the end of August, Edin Dzeko provided City fans with a display that few probably expected.

White Hart Lane was the venue and the Bosnian striker produced a perfect hat trick. He opened the scoring with his right foot, before producing a brilliant header to double City's lead. Early in the second half, he converted Yaya Toure's low ball into the box with his left foot. The only way to improve on that is with a goal of the month contender from the edge of the box, so that's exactly what he did – after Aguero had got his customary league goal.

The biggest dent to United's goal difference, however, occurred on 23 October 2011. With City on top of the league by two points, victory in the Manchester derby would lift United back to the summit. Perhaps the Reds were arrogant, being at home. Perhaps City's history of defeats in the fixture and United's performance in the Community Shield had added to that.

But City blew them away.

Despite being under pressure for most of the opening stages, City soon got a foothold in the game following a moment when David Silva (somehow) kept possession in the United area with five defenders around him. Yaya Toure blazed over. Then Mario Balotelli rolled a shot into the corner of the net.

A red card for Jonny Evans early in the second half helped put the second nail into United's coffin. City were dominating possession, exactly as they had done all season, by stretching the play and giving short, accurate passes in little triangles all over the pitch. Aside from the odd breakaway, the game was being played in the United half and it was the hosts on the back foot.

Goals two and three, from Balotelli and, of course, Aguero, virtually secured the win. A late fightback was almost on the cards, as Darren Fletcher pulled a goal back, with arguably the best strike of the day. Though that will be little consolation to the home side, as City dented United's

---

Manchester United 1-6 Manchester City
Sunday 23 October 2011, Premier League

City: Hart, Richards, Kompany (c), Lescott, Clichy, Barry, Y Toure, Milner (Kolarov 89), Silva, Aguero (Nasri 75), Balotelli (Dzeko 70)
Goals: Balotelli (22, 60), Aguero (69), Dzeko (89, 90+3), Silva (90+1)

The trip to Old Trafford is one of the first the fans look for when the fixtures are announced in the summer. In the build-up to this game, the two sides had already met in the Community Shield and that had been another United last minute winner. Neither set of fans was expected what happened that Sunday.

City – the better side for all but the opening 20 minutes – demolished United on their own patch, inflicting the heaviest defeat the Reds had ever suffered in the Premier League. Critics argued the gap between the sides was narrowing.

But, as the goals went in, City fans argued the opposite. They claimed it was getting wider and that it was the Blues who were pulling away. That idea would turn out to be premature, but given the result, you could hardly blame the fans for getting excited.

---

goal difference and boosted their own to the tune of three more – thanks to Dzeko, Silva and then Dzeko again. That game caused a swing of ten goals, adding five to City's goal difference and taking five from United's.

As the goals went in during City's start to the season, the records fell. With each passing game without defeat – the first of which came in December – more years were added to the statistic that said it was the club's best ever start since...

Following the 3-1 home win over Newcastle in November, the club had made the best ever start to a Premier League season, winning 11 and drawing the other of their 12 opening games. Arsenal's Invincibles had previously held the record, with nine wins and three draws.

It had been almost half a century since any club had scored as many as City had in their opening 12 matches; Tottenham scored 44 in the beginning of 1963-64, compared to City's 42 in 2011-12. Compared with that stage the season before, the club was 27 goals and 13 points better off. The records tumbled week by week.

It seems churlish to simply dismiss the high volume of goals City scored in those four months as a result of the opposition suffering tired legs. Perhaps it's brutal to come to this conclusion, but of course that was the case – it wouldn't surprise me for that to have been part of Roberto Mancini's plan. He was a fan of possession football; the opposition chase the ball for large spells of the game and they are tired out. City keep the ball and the work is easy. Cue the ruthless finish, as goals galore are added.

Fans previously were frustrated by City's insistence on playing sideways and backwards. Under previous managers it was seemingly down to a lack of cutting edge, but under Mancini it was more because, in roughly 30 passes' time, the sideways and backwards ball movement will have got the opposition left back out of position and give the team a

Attacking Flair and Movement

Throughout the 2011-12 season, you'd have been forgiven for thinking that City didn't have a gameplan. Pundits seemed to believe that Roberto Mancini had his defence set up as he'd done in previous campaigns, simply adding a pile of forwards to score the goals, with little care for actual tactical input.

And that's not true. Yes, the players up front probably needed very little direction, but there was a clear game-plan and it all boiled down to one word: movement.

Mancini had several setups for the forward players, his favourite being two strikers with two attacking midfielders in behind. However, these positions weren't set in stone, with the principle being that it's impossible to man-mark a player out of the game if he keeps swapping positions with another.

So, when Silva cropped up on the right, Aguero would drift out to the left, or when Dzeko came deep to collect the ball, Nasri would roam further forward into space. Throw in some overlapping runs from the fullbacks and it was organised chaos in the opposition box – with City doing the organising.

Another tactic Mancini enjoyed in the opening stages of the campaign was the "dare you to attack us" strategy, mainly when defending corners. He stuck with his zonal marking system, but neglected three areas of the box, in order to leave three attacking players on the halfway line. Naturally, the opposition would have a choice to make – send the centre-backs forward to attack and risk the counter, or keep four men back to cover the likes of Aguero, Silva and Balotelli lurking by the centre-circle.

This was seemingly less successful, however, as Mancini quickly resorted to marking the whole box and soon the clean sheet count rose.

chance of an opening. One lady, who shall remain nameless (largely because I don't know her name), who sits near me at Eastlands once remarked that City were only "doing this to see how many passes they can make!" I'm sure she felt daft when Brad Friedel, then of Aston Villa, picked the ball out of his net without one of his team having touched the ball in around three minutes, as Mario Balotelli tapped it in.

David Silva

Born: 8 Jan 1986
Signed: 30 Jun 2010
Sold: -

Apps: 127 (16 sub)
Goals: 19
Yellow Cards: 6
Red Cards: 0
Notes: Kisses a tattoo of his cousin Cynthia's name on his wrist when he scores, after she passed away from cancer aged just three.

So it can come as little surprise that most of City's goals had been second half strikes. Teams with fresh legs can recover mistakes quickly. When those legs have chased the ball for 70-odd minutes, suddenly it's not as easy, as the likes of Norwich, Blackburn and indeed Manchester United found out all too well.

City's only defeat in the 2011 bit of the 2011-12 season came at Stamford Bridge, in a game that could have gone very differently. A goal from Mario Balotelli in the 2nd minute should have been followed up by a penalty – probably from the Italian – but the referee missed a clear foul on David Silva. Following that City did something they hadn't done for a long time. They lost their cool.

A cute tactical adjustment by then-Chelsea boss Andre Villas-Boas gave the home side more ball possession and before the visitors could realise it, they had lost control of the game, falling under heavy pressure. Then came the equaliser and there was little the away side could do to wrestle the game back, especially following Gael Clichy's entirely avoidable red card for two bookable offences. A late penalty won the game for the hosts.

It made up three of the nine points the Blues dropped before the turn of the New Year. It was a blip in an otherwise flawless campaign so far.

Throughout this remarkable season opening, City had another challenge to face: the Champions League. Having been drawn in an awfully difficult group, the Blues had made hard work of beating Villarreal at home, following a draw with Napoli and a defeat to Bayern Munich. Back-to-back victories over the Spanish club, however, left City in a good position to qualify, though defeat in Italy put paid to that dream. Despite a final night home win over the eventual runners up, City finished third in the group with a points total that would have seen them qualify from all but one of the other groups.

Champions League Group A

8 December 2011

		W	D	L	Pts
1	Bayern Munich	4	1	1	13
2	Napoli	3	2	1	11
3	Man City	3	1	2	10
4	Villarreal	0	0	6	0

Throw in some midweek League Cup matches and suddenly City's start to the campaign seemed remarkable. There seemed to be little effect on the squad, perhaps due to an element of rotation by the manager, but probably more down to momentum. Premier League teams were beginning to fear facing the would-be Champions. Coming away from the Etihad with a 2-0 defeat was a plus point, given some of the beatings others had taken there – and, as much as the fans might not want to admit it, the Blues were finally benefiting from the fear factor that had troubled most visitors to Old Trafford in the last two decades. City had had few problems picking off teams who had packed their defences.

Another season too soon? Not this time. This was a club hell bent on being the best in the country.

Chapter Seven
The Bogey Teams

THROUGHOUT HIS TIME AT MANCHESTER City, Roberto Mancini couldn't crack several things: the now infamous 3-5-2 system (which we'll come on to later on), the month of March and the Stadium Of Light. Indeed, it was New Year's Day 2012 that was tinted with both joy and frustration for me: joy as the second series of the BBC's brilliant drama *Sherlock* began with a wonderful story involving the delightful Irene Adler; frustration as, once again, City went to Sunderland to dominate possession and chances, but left with a defeat, thanks to a goal from Ji with roughly half a second remaining when the ball crossed the line.

Having watched the game on television, awaiting my New Year meal of chicken tikka cooked by my father, I remained numb on the sofa. City had been on level points atop the Premier League with United, but had played a game fewer – with the Reds having lost to Blackburn at Old Trafford the day before. It was a missed opportunity. At the time, it was easy to dismiss as a 'free defeat', given that City's main title rivals had lost before kick-off, there was no way the Blues could have fallen behind. Still, it was annoying not to have taken advantage of the slip up.

But there was something about the Black Cats that Mancini could never crack, especially away from home. His first ever trip to the Stadium of Light left his side needing an Adam Johnson special to level it up in the last seconds of the match. He visited three more times – and each time he dominated the game, but lost by one goal to nil.

Stadium of Light

Premier League Record:
P9 W4 D1 L4 F11 A7

Roberto Mancini Record:
P4 W0 D1 L3 F1 A4

In 2010-11, it was the third league match of the season. Having drawn at Tottenham and battered Liverpool, the Blues rocked up in the north-east with a fair amount of confidence. Tevez missed an open goal, Adebayor had a glorious opportunity saved from inside the six-yard box and then Richards gave away a needless penalty in second half stoppage time. It was converted and even the introduction of Jo wasn't enough to pull the scoreline level in the final seconds.

A year on and the trip came on New Year's Day. Dzeko forced a point-blank save from Mignolet, Nasri had a shot cleared off the line, Richards and Dzeko both had efforts hit the bar and then Ji carried the ball around Joe Hart to score the winner. The home side had barely left their half, there was an offside in the build-up and there wasn't even enough time for the visitors to shoot from kick-off. Sometimes everything just

Adam Johnson

Born: 14 Jul 1987
Signed: 1 Feb 2010
Sold: 24 Aug 2012

Apps: 54 (43 sub)
Goals: 15
Yellow Cards: 4
Red Cards: 0
Notes: Has scored against City twice – once before and once after signing for the Blues.

stacks up against you.

Mancini's fourth and final trip to Wearside was at a similar time of year to the third, coming this time on Boxing Day 2012. Given the Blues' record there and the very fact that they had, in the course of their summer transfers, sold Adam Johnson to their opposition, there was only ever going to be one outcome. There was controversy in the build-up, with Pablo Zabaleta sure he was fouled, but a long-range effort from Johnson towards Joe Hart's near post should have been stopped. It wasn't and, though it wasn't another last-gasp goal, it was a second half strike that would turn out to be the winner in another 1-0 for the home side.

In 2012, the New Year's Day defeat to Sunderland started a spell where City became vulnerable. Suddenly the team that had been free-scoring for all of the four and a half months previous couldn't buy a goal, and two shutouts in two games over the Christmas period had been a concern. The free-flowing attacking football had been toned down somewhat, with one of the most notable

2011-12 PL Goals Scored

August - December:
18 games, 53 goals

January - May:
18 games, 40 goals

changes coming in how the team defended corners. Previously, they had left three men on the half-way line as a kind of 'dare' to the opposition. It was as if Roberto Mancini was saying: "Yes, you might have a chance to score from this corner, but in leaving Aguero, Silva and Nasri on the half-way line, you're going to have to take a huge risk if you want to send your centre-backs forward." Suddenly, it was everybody in the City box to mark their zones. The emphasis had switched from securing a big win, to simply securing a win: as the old saying goes, points win prizes. And Mancini wanted the points.

While the season got back on track with a home win over Liverpool, things were clearly not as slick as they had been before. City looked groggy against the Reds until a Pepe Reina error gifted the home side a goal. Then the next two matches were to end in defeat again, as a controversial red card ended Vincent Kompany's FA Cup campaign after just 12 minutes and City slipped 3-0 down to United. Two second half goals almost sparked a comeback, but the home side fell just short. However, when Liverpool returned for the first leg of the League Cup semi final, City put up little fight at all, allowing Steven Gerrard to score a first half penalty to win the match.

City's troubled period didn't end there. Before going out of the League Cup at Anfield, the Blues struggled to overcome relegation-threatened Wigan at the DW Stadium, winning thanks to a set piece goal via the head of Edin Dzeko. The next weekend, Tottenham came to the Etihad, with a view of keeping their own title challenge alive. Having been two goals up, City took their foot off the gas and allowed the visitors back into the match within a matter of ten minutes of opening the scoring and going in front. It really should have been Tottenham who stole the points, as Defoe missed a sitter in the far reaches of stoppage time, but a long punt forward won City a penalty and Mario Balotelli converted. It really was a steal.

The City fans had already written off the club's next fixture. In fact, ask any City fan for a prediction of what will happen when the Blues travel to Goodison Park and you'll get the same answer every time. It's usually two words long and the second one is 'off'. Aside from the year Mark Hughes' City decided to take all three points there –

Goodison Park

Premier League Record:
P16 W2 D4 L10 F12 A23

Roberto Mancini Record:
P4 W0 D0 L4 F1 A7

you know, the year the club only won two away games and they were at the two bogey grounds in Sunderland and Everton – City's record on Merseyside was, to put it mildly, abysmal. It got to the stage where the fans probably wouldn't have complained if we'd just skipped actually playing the fixture each year and awarded the points to the Toffees, but apparently that's against the laws of the game.

Spoilsports at the FA, I tell you.

While it was widely hoped that things might have changed, a 1-0 defeat at Goodison Park was hardly unexpected. It's always interesting to see how the goal will come that defeats City on these occasions and, this year, it had been a deflected effort that left the goalkeeper standing. It's usually that or a wonder strike.

It had been around this time that I had started a new job. For reasons I still don't understand, a Premier League club based in London use a media company in Manchester to film their reserve team and academy games in order to make the highlights packages that go on their website. It was my job to travel with the cameraman to their youth matches and write down everything that happened that might be worthy of the highlights reel for the editors back in the north. It was also my responsibility to make sure the footage had been transferred from the camera to the company's laptop. The main cameraman I was working with was an Evertonian.

He'd noted a change in attitude towards Manchester City from the Everton team and speculated that it was down to David Moyes. Perhaps he was still displeased with losing Joleon Lescott or perhaps it dated back to when he was Preston boss and Kevin Keegan signed Jon Macken. Another Everton fan I know and who I went to university with suggests that Moyes was a "cantankerous, old Scot" who simply "doesn't like City" – also a possibility and I think, given how much the Toffees have raised their game against the Blues in the past, City's fans feel pretty much the same way towards Everton.

The job, however, was causing me to lose my Saturday mornings. Most of the youth team fixtures were 11 o'clock kick-offs in London, meaning I had to meet the cameraman about five hours earlier. We'd drive down, film the game, do the post-match interview and drive back. Often in time for me to catch City – usually because they weren't on the traditional Saturday 3 o'clock kick-off slot.

Throughout February, it was fine. I didn't miss a minute of football and City won all of their five games, conceding just once – in the Europa League to FC Porto. Fulham and Blackburn provided two comfortable 3-0 victories, even if the quality of the football City played was still nowhere near to the standard of the season's opening months. A trip to Villa Park ended with a very nervy 1-0 win, though this was the attitude of champions, right? Going somewhere, not being at their best, yet still coming away with the points?

But then the month of March happened.

Roberto Mancini's first ever March at City in 2010 saw two wins: a battling performance at home to Wigan, which was affected by a red card to one of the visiting defenders, and a hard-fought 2-1 triumph at Craven Cottage, in a game that will be forever remembered as the day that Roque Santa Cruz scored his final goal for

March 2010
Sunderland 1-1 Man City
Fulham 1-2 Man City
Man City 0-2 Everton
Man City 3-0 Wigan

March 2011
Man City 1-0 Wigan
Chelsea 2-0 Man City

March 2012
Man City 2-0 Bolton
Swansea 1-0 Man City
Man City 2-1 Chelsea
Stoke 1-1 Man City
Man City 3-3 Sunderland

March 2013
Aston Villa 0-1 Man City
Everton 2-0 Man City
Man City 4-0 Newcastle

City. The other matches ended in a draw and a defeat – and it will come as no surprise to you when I say the two team names: Sunderland and Everton.

Results were better in the Italian's second month of March, however the performances did leave something to be desired. Ok, so the Blues battered Aston Villa in the FA Cup in 2011, but 1-0 home wins over Wigan, Dynamo Kiev (which wasn't enough to see the club through into the next round of the Europa League thanks to an awful performance in the away leg earlier in the month) and Reading were unconvincing at best. And then the month was rounded off by a 0-2 defeat at Chelsea, in another match where City never looked like scoring.

Things did improve in Roberto Mancini's final March of his City career. A 5-0 drubbing of Barnsley in the FA Cup helped matters, as did a four goal battering of Newcastle. Though, yet again, there was an unconvincing away win at a relegation-threatened side in Aston Villa – with the Blues only winning thanks to an error seized upon by Edin Dzeko. And then there was, of course, the customary defeat at Goodison Park.

But, as I was travelling up and down the M6 during March 2012, I was finding myself needing to come up with excuse after excuse for my team's poor performances. The would-be champions went into the month on the top of the Premier League table, two points clear of United in second place. They finished it having slipped into second, now trailing the Reds by five points – a seven point swing over five matches.

The victory over Bolton was a more difficult one than it should have been, though City created enough chances to have won the game three times over. A quick exit from the Europa League, thanks to two away goals conceded at the Etihad and a 1-0 defeat in Lisbon, was either side of one of the worst performances of the season. City travelled to

Swansea for the first time ever in the Premier League and, despite a 4-0 opening weekend victory, the away side rarely threatened. A Stefan Savic mistake allowed the home side a chance to score, which they duly took with eight minutes to play. One City fan was famously photographed crying after the game.

"There is still a long way to go," I told the cameraman. "We've still got to play United yet," I'd say to one of the journalists I was working with. They might have believed my confidence, but I didn't believe it myself. City were leaking points and slipping off the pace. The early season performances had been a thing of the past and it felt like an ice age since the club had been blowing the opposition out

---

Manchester City 2-1 Chelsea
Wednesday 21 March 2012, Premier League

City: Hart, Zabaleta, Richards (c), K Toure, Clichy, de Jong (Tevez 66), Y Toure, Silva (Dzeko 77), Nasri, Aguero, Balotelli (Barry 45)
Goals: Aguero (pen 78), Nasri (85)

When City really needed a win to keep up with United at the top of the table, a visit from Chelsea to the Etihad wasn't the ideal fixture to be facing. However, despite starting the better, the Blues couldn't force a breakthrough and it was left to a fortunate strike from Gary Cahill to give the visitors the lead – Kolo Toure could have done more to clear, and the Chelsea defender's shot deflected off both Toure brothers to deceive the stranded Joe Hart. Crisis.

However, the was hope with 12 minutes to play: a needless handball gave Aguero the chance to equalise from the spot. He scored and grabbed the ball; there was no time now for any celebrations.

Seven minutes on Tevez's return to first team action won the game. His neat reverse ball to complete a one-two with Nasri allowed the Frenchman to chip Cech. Crisis averted.

---

of the water.

A home win with Chelsea quickly got the club back on track, though the performance at the Britannia Stadium left something to be desired. Peter Crouch did what he does best and arrived to score an important goal against City. This time he took on an outrageous volley to beat Joe Hart with just under an hour played. Yaya Toure salvaged a point with an equally stunning long-range drive and it did put the Blues back on top of the league, but only on goal difference and they had played one more game than United, who then went on to beat Fulham two days later.

I rolled the excuses out the following Saturday morning, but, as time ran out on City's season, they were filled with less and less conviction. That week, City had a rare Saturday 3 o'clock kick off. Heavy traffic on the journey home had meant that I hadn't got back to my car – parked in a layby just off the M6 – until the game had begun. Still having to get the laptop back to the necessary people, I hurried to get back to Manchester, listening to City's match on the radio.

It was at home to Sunderland.

It had been the away trips to the Black Cats that had been the problem for Roberto Mancini, but this fixture was proving problematic. A slow start had led to the visitors taking the lead. BBC Radio 5 Live suddenly told me there was a penalty at the Etihad Stadium and quickly Balotelli converted it to level the score. I performed a mini-fist pump as I exited the motorway and joined Princess Parkway.

Immediately, Sunderland pulled another goal ahead through Nicklas Bendtner – and, should any of my friends from university be reading this, I'd like to say that he's a great player who only ever scores against great clubs and any mickey taking I may have done about his time with Arsenal was completely ironic.

I dropped the laptop off and the second half began as I

got back into the car. Still fully intending to drive to the stadium, park up and run to get in for the final half hour, I took the Mancunian Way and headed for Gorton Road. I spotted a space, and, just as I was about to begin reversing into it, Sunderland added a third goal.

I drove home. It was the first time I could have got there in time to see the end of a game and I chose not to.

As I got to my house, there were around 6 minutes of the match left. At 3-1 down and with City's title bid seemingly going up in smoke, I was in no mood for jokes, so seeing that the cameraman I had been with in the morning had sent me a text wasn't the best thing that could happen to improve it. I dared to look at it: "Sunderland fans doing the Poznan," it said. "Oh dear." I threw the phone at the sofa in pure anger (which, in case my dad – who now owns the mobile – was wondering, is why there's a small chunk missing from the bottom left

---

Manchester City 3-3 Sunderland
Saturday 31 March 2012
Premier League

City: Hart, Richards (A Johnson 45), Kompany (c), K Toure, Kolarov, de Jong, Y Toure, Silva (Tevez 58), Milner (Pizarro 80), Balotelli, Dzeko
Goals: Balotelli (pen 44, 85), Kolarov (86)

Going into the game, City hadn't lost at home all season. In fact, when it came to league games, they hadn't dropped a single point, having won all 15 home matches. The fans were full of confidence.

Yet City just didn't turn up. They fought back from a goal down only to fall behind again immediately. It took two late goals from nothing from Balotelli and Kolarov to earn a point. The influence of Pizarro in the final ten minutes was what made the difference.

In the context of the game, it was a good point; in the context of the season, however, it didn't seem like it was good enough.

---

corner of it).

Two late goals rescued the result, but a late draw was surely not enough at this stage in the season. It was a good point to have fought back and won, but equally, it wasn't good enough. Sunderland would become the only team City didn't beat in the Premier League at home that season.

Throw in a 1-0 defeat at Arsenal in the first game of April and, with just six games to go, the team that had looked like they would steamroller over the division a matter of three months earlier, had fallen eight points off the pace at top of the table. Roberto Mancini's bogey teams and problems in the month of March had been a harsh kick to the knackers.

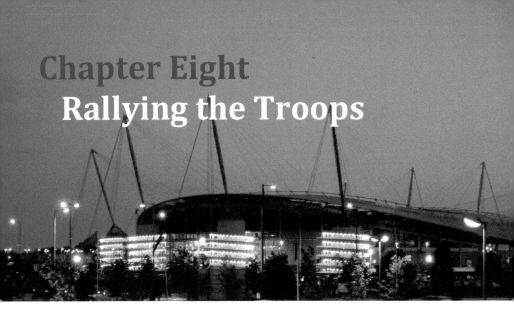

Chapter Eight
Rallying the Troops

ERE'S THE THING; I'M A defensive kind of chap. Perhaps it's part of my nature having grown up as a Manchester City supporter that I'll always try to protect my lot and defend it to the hilt, because – if I don't – there's always the likelihood that it's going to be destroyed, burnt to the ground and then steamrollered for good measure. Applying that logic to football, when leading by a goal it's my natural reaction to try to make sure we don't concede. Some managers like to go in for the kill and try and get their team out of sight. Personally, I'd have ten men on the line blocking anything that even thought about coming near to the goal, while the goalkeeper began building a brick wall between the posts.

Though that would only be an option in the second half. Tactically, I'd be an idiot to suggest bricking up a goal that my team would be shooting at after the break.

However, this defensive nature of mine has also led to a 'damage limitation' sort of mentality. And, in order to avoid being ribbed too much by my non-City supporting friends, I'd thrown the towel in on the Blues' title bid after the 1-1 draw at Stoke. "Oh, well," I'd say. "It just wasn't our season."

This was despite knowing full well is should have been.

So, when it was a confirmed full time result that City had drawn at home to Sunderland, I was forced to pick another towel out of the cupboard just so I could throw it into the ring again, because that was an afternoon when a lot of fans conceded that their club had blown it. Nevertheless, it simply confirmed my position that it was all over.

Roll on Sunday 8 April 2012. The day that began with Manchester United taking a controversial 2-0 home win over Queens Park Rangers ended with Manchester City whimpering to a 1-0 away defeat at Arsenal. Knowing that their title rivals had won earlier in the day had heaped pressure on the Blues in a match that was already difficult enough. They'd never won at the Emirates in the league, having scored just one Premier League goal there since it opened in 2006. Roberto Mancini had masterminded two goalless draws there – thanks largely to defending like I said I'd do earlier in the chapter. But that wouldn't be enough this time.

Game 32:

Arsenal 1-0 Man City

Man Utd 2-0 QPR

		W	D	L	GD	Pts
1	Man Utd	25	4	3	51	79
2	Man City	22	5	5	49	71

And the club did what they traditionally do best when needing to win. They lost.

A goal by Mikel Arteta left the Blues eight points off the top of the table with just six matches left. Throughout the season, when both City and United had played level games, the gap had never been more than five points. This was the biggest it had been and this was when a whole industrial-sized laundry basket full of towels joined mine in the ring. There were a few still clinging on to the hope, but many cynics like me were lambasting the return of the good ol' typical Manchester City.

We thought it was consigned to the history books. Instead, it had been like the school bully, waiting around the corner and ready to wedgie us when we least expected it. And boy did it catch us unawares.

By the time I had done the post mortem that evening on *Blue Moon Live*, I was feeling at ease with the club's fate. In a strange way, actually being forced to talk about the bad stuff on the radio helps to speed up the personal recovery from the defeat – if a game's been bad, we have to say so, but we do it by analysing what went wrong. For some reason, that's like the methadone to the addiction of supporting City.

And following the on-air therapy session, I was quite relaxed about the eight points and six games thing. It virtually sent a sledgehammer through the windscreen of belief that City could recover the position and I was comfortable, if not happy, with that. The season was over, so we might as well just enjoy the ending to it.

Following

Game 33:					
Man City 4-0 West Brom					
Wigan 1-0 Man Utd					
		W	D	L	GD	Pts
1 Man Utd		25	4	4	50	79
2 Man City		23	5	5	53	74

the Arsenal defeat, Roberto Mancini commented that anything was possible in football and that it wasn't over until it was over. Though he quickly changed his tune, deciding that (publically, if not privately to his staff and players) the title race was over. No matter what happened, he concluded that "it is finished" and United had won it.

Three days later, one of the worst things that could have happened for my emotions happened. City gave West Brom a good hiding at the Etihad while relegation threatened Wigan continued their imperious march to survival by conquering United at the DW. The result was confirmed via the big screens and suddenly, with five games to go, the gap was back down to five points. And in the back of my head, a flicker of hope re-appeared.

Ask any Manchester City fan down the years and they'll tell you that that's the worst bit. There's the despair of the continued failures of the team and there's the elation that goes with the successes, each of them are easy to deal with. But what does get to supporters more than perhaps any other club's fans is the dangling carrot of belief so often held aloft in front of Blues, that, no matter how unlikely it is, things might be getting better. And the truth is, they might be. That doesn't mean the fans can deal with the hope any easier, though.

Despite the gap having been reduced by three points, the party line coming from the club remained the same: we'll focus on our games and if the gap closes further, then great. If it doesn't, it doesn't. Oh – and United have already won the league.

The next weekend, the points gap stayed the same (though City did add one more to their goal difference advantage). The Blues travelled to Carrow Road and, seemingly still playing without the burden of having to chase down the league leaders, ripped Norwich a new one as a game of 'anything you can do I can do better' between City's two front men errupted. Seriously: Tevez belted one in from long range, so Aguero pulled off one of the

Game 34:
Norwich 1-6 Man City
Man Utd 4-0 Aston Villa

Game 35:
Wolves 0-2 Man City
Man Utd 4-4 Everton

		W	D	L	GD	Pts
1	Man Utd	26	5	4	54	83
2	Man City	25	5	5	60	80

best volleys of the season; Aguero scored a beauty of a solo goal having beaten half of the Norwich team, so Tevez secured a hat-trick.

Maybe if the Argentine duo had been playing together all season, the bizarre one-upmanship they had going might have fired them both (and City) to league winners by the end of March. Ok, so, I might have exaggerated somewhat there.

With four games to go and five points to catch up, few City fans believed it would happen. It didn't matter that the Blues took on United because, unless they slipped up elsewhere, they would still be able to take the league on points. Except on the afternoon of Sunday 22 April 2012, the situation changed and it was roles reversed from the fortnight before. Again United played first and City second, but knowing that a win would leave them eight points ahead of their rivals (having played a game more) with three matches left, the Reds fluffed their lines somewhat.

City fans the world over tuned in to watch Everton take the lead at Old Trafford. With no love lost between City fans and Everton, it was an unsettling feeling. They were doing us a favour. That wasn't right.

Order was quickly restored. Less than ten minutes after the away side opened the scoring, the home side equalised and, despite the United performance being below par and Everton being the better team, many City fans sighed that inevitable sigh and accepted it was all just a pipe dream. This feeling doubled when United made it 2-1, then 3-1 within the space of three more second half minutes.

But the cruel world of hope hadn't finished with those City fans just yet. It conspired to fill their hearts once again, as Marouane Fellaini pulled a goal back for the visitors. Maybe they might snatch something? That thought lasted all of two minutes, until Wayne Rooney got his second of the match and cancelled out the Belgian's goal, immediately making it 4-2.

And, as I headed upstairs to sulk until the City match came on the TV, I heard Everton pull another goal back for 4-3. I was getting sick of this hope visitor, especially if it was going to leave fairly quickly. But this time, the visitor hung around and, with five minutes of the game remaining, it poured itself a cup of hot tea and settled in for the afternoon, as Steven Pienaar equalised. I remained upstairs, convinced of another last-minute United heartbreak, as they always seemed to do to City.

It never came and it finished 4-4.

I texted the cameraman who I had been working with the words 'Thank you very much!' It turned out he was filming a rugby match that day and hadn't been able to check the result. When he could finally reply, he thought I was being sarcastic and that Everton had rolled over for the Reds. I was deadly serious.

That result meant that a win at Wolves would ensure City would go into the Manchester derby just three points behind their rivals. The side-effect was that a win for the visitors that day would have relegated the hosts, a team with fans that it was generally agreed had been let down by a series of bad decisions at the club. Before the game, Roberto Mancini continued to toe the party line: United's draw didn't let City back into the title race. No, it made the Blues' job harder, since the gap had been five points and now it was six. It was said with his tongue firmly in his cheek, but it worked, as Sergio Aguero and Samir Nasri did the business.

And for the next eight days, I began to feel worse and worse about the impending Manchester derby. I considered running away, changing my name and living abroad, but then I realised that that plan was doomed to fail, given my inability to go longer than a couple of hours without updating Twitter. I had no choice but to wait for kick off, nearly throw up several times and let the nerves take hold.

Once again, Manchester City were ruining me.

The situation was simple: win and City would go back to the top of the table on goal difference. From then on in, providing United didn't win their remaining games by eight more goals than City did and that City won their remaining two games, the Blues would lift the title. A draw in the derby would leave United needing a win and a draw from their final two matches. A defeat, however, would leave the Reds needing just a draw. It was win or bust for City.

Game 36:
Man City 1-0 Man Utd

		W	D	L	GD	Pts
1	Man City	26	5	5	61	83
2	Man Utd	26	5	5	53	83

The conservative side of me completely understood where Manchester United manager Sir Alex Ferguson was coming from when he named his starting line-up for that game at the Etihad. His team had the advantage in the league and there was no sense in risking the Blues winning the game by making it full of fast, free-flowing football. That's how City had performed best, so there was little reason why the Reds would allow them to do it. Their best bet was to kill the game at kick off.

However, Roberto Mancini wasn't simply going into the game with a gung-ho attitude. In truth, it would have been suicidal to City's title chances. He needed to be

Vincent Kompany

Born: 10 Apr 1986
Signed: 22 Aug 2008
Sold: -

Apps: 198 (8 sub)
Clean Sheets: 78
Goals: 7
Yellow Cards: 37
Red Cards: 3
Notes: Premier League player of the season in 2012.

coy and bide his time. United came out of the traps quickly, while City grew into the game, slowly strangled it and, in the end, didn't allow United a shot on target in the whole 90 minutes. It was left for Vincent Kompany to head home from a David Silva corner to give the hosts the lead, and it was the captain's goal that was enough to win the match.

Though, throughout the duration stoppage time, it did feel like the fourth official had indicated five added minutes but the referee had chosen to play 55. When the whistle finally blew, the amount of tension released from the ground would have needed an axe to cut through, let alone a knife. City were back on top of the table and back in control of the title race.

So, when it came to the penultimate game of the season at St James' Park, City had the odd position of playing first in the day. And this meant that they were being put under a hypothetical pressure, where they couldn't take anything for granted and need the Reds to slip up. By this stage, Roberto Mancini's team selection was no surprise – he had been going unchanged with his strongest starting eleven since losing at the Emirates.

Just after the hour mark, Mancini made a tactical reshuffle that had been familiar to City fans, but was publically lauded as one of the best substitutions in Premier League history. In truth, it was a move he had pulled before, but to those who didn't regularly see the Blues, it could have

Game 37:

Newcastle 0-2 Man City

Man Utd 2-0 Swansea

		W	D	L	GD	Pts
1	Man City	27	5	5	63	86
2	Man Utd	27	5	5	55	86

seemed like an odd one. At 0-0 and desperate for a win, he pulled the creative Samir Nasri from the pitch and added the defensive midfielder Nigel de Jong. Baffling, right?

Unleashing Yaya Toure

Roberto Mancini's substitutions frequently raised more than an eyebrow from the watching public, yet the Italian had a clear gameplan with each and evey one of them – even if it wasn't conventional. Observers often criticised his decision not to simply throw as many strikers onto the pitch as possible when City were chasing a goal, but there is a logic to removing a striker for, say, a midfielder when a goal down. The teams needs more ball possession – it's impossible to score without the ball, and adding more strikers will simply leave more players isolated up front.

One of Mancini's biggest substitutions – and we saw it regularly towards the end of the 2011-12 season – was to do exactly that: bring a midfielder on for a striker when chasing a goal. This was because he had the destructive power of Yaya Toure moving forward. If the opposition didn't stop a Toure run inside its first five yards, then he was going to finish his run whether their defenders liked it or not.

That change made it possible for City to win the league, as it was that move at Newcastle the swung the balance of power in the game and got City their two vital goals, both of them coming from the Ivorian pushing forward. His bursts – against the tired legs of the defenders – were impossible to deal with, and it was enough to overpower the Magpies.

Well, no. City fans had seen it several times before. The creative talent had spent two-thirds of the game tiring out the opposition defence and now, with a new holding midfielder added to the game, the raw power of Yaya Toure could be unleashed. Several times in the final third of that match did Toure burst away from Newcastle defenders and cause the home side problems.

It was a mere eight minutes after the substitution that it paid off. Toure himself nestled the ball into the bottom corner of Krul's net from the edge of the box, from a position that he wouldn't have been in had the change not been made. And then, as the home side pressed, he broke away again and should have doubled his tally, but he slipped at the vital moment in trying to round the goalkeeper.

Instead, he forced City's fans to go through several more heart attacks as the home side got closer and closer to levelling the score – save for one of the blocks of the season from Micah Richards.

The home side were getting nearer. That was until the Blues cleared a corner and, via Nigel de Jong and Gael Clichy on the break, Yaya Toure found space in the box to finish off the match, taking an age to get his shot away, but seeming like he had all the time in the world.

Micah Richards

Born: 24 Jun 1988
Signed: Academy, 2005
Sold: -

Apps: 218 (16 sub)
Clean Sheets: 81
Goals: 9
Yellow Cards: 32
Red Cards: 0
Notes: Swore on live TV after equalising in stoppage time in the FA Cup at Aston Villa in just his fourth appearance for the club.

Come full time, that tactical switch had the away end singing 'We're going to win the league'.

You'd have thought that history would have taught City's fans not to presume the simple job would be done. Ok, so the Blues were at home on the final day of the season, where they had dropped just two points in the other 18 league fixtures. And it was relegation candidates Queens Park Rangers who would be the opposition.

Nevertheless, thinking it was already over when Manchester City are concerned is very dangerous.

It's City. Anything can happen.

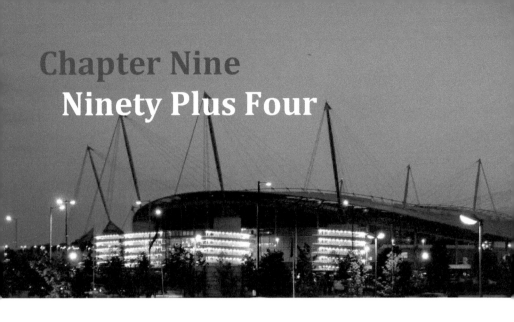

Chapter Nine
Ninety Plus Four

THERE WAS A SPRING IN my step on the morning of Sunday 13 May 2012. Normally, having to get up at 6.30am on a Sunday for work leaves me in a groggily unhappy mood, though there was a smile on my face as I steamed down the motorway that day. How could I not be happy? City were going to win their first top division title in 44 years, their second trophy in my lifetime and ABSOLUTELY NOTHING WHATSOEVER was going to go wrong – and that was a guarantee.

The winning mentality that Roberto Mancini had talked about giving the club when he first arrived was evidently weaved into the DNA these days. Manchester City under previous managers wouldn't have overcome that eight point gap over six games – well, under six games, given the blues went back to the top after just four. Given the club's home record and the task in front of them, plus how the team and the fans believed in themselves under one of their most successful managers, meant this match felt like a formality. No, it was a formality.

As I arrived home from work, I munched my lunch and eagerly awaited setting off for the Etihad. I had my handheld recording device with me, ready to take the opinions of several fans for the radio once the trophy had been lifted. We arrived to the ground early. If you know our family, you'll know this never happens. Every single Mooney will be late to their own funeral, it's the way we're built.

The teams came out of the tunnel and, all of a sudden, I was nervous beyond belief. I couldn't stand still, shifting my weight from one foot to the other. I just wanted the game to get underway, so City could score and we could call it a day, lift the trophy and enjoy the evening. Looking back now, I feel silly at how naïve I was in thinking it would be so easy.

It didn't start particularly well. QPR had come to the Etihad – with a former manager, too – seemingly to go home with a point. That would have been enough for them to be sure of Premier League survival, so they were set up to try and get that. And the home side struggled to break through, with Paddy Kenny in goal not being called into too much action.

Then news from Sunderland: United had taken the lead thanks to Wayne Rooney. That goal had put the reds on top of the table as things stood. City simply had to match or better United's result, while United had to hope that they bettered City's. Right now, the latter was happening.

City had been camped in the QPR half for most of the first period and I remember thinking that the breakthrough might never come. Despite the home side's attacking flair, it's difficult to produce much when there were 11 opposition players inside their own area. And, to my eyes, it got worse, as Yaya Toure seemingly pulled a hamstring as he tried to play a ball over the top. There'd be no bursting runs forward at a time when they might have been vital.

Though clearly in some pain and in a fair bit of discomfort, the Ivorian remained on the pitch. And, just minutes before half time, he assisted City's opening goal and Pablo Zabaleta scored his first of the season. It was a strike that everybody – including Zabaleta himself – thought had been saved. And then everybody – including Zabaleta again – thought it had missed. And then, somehow, it was in the net, as Paddy Kenny had bizarrely pushed the shot up into the air and over the line via the right-hand post. It didn't make much sense, but it was enough to put City back on the top, even if it negated the laws of physics for a brief moment.

Manchester City 3-2 Queens Park Rangers
Sunday 13 May 2012, Premier League

City: Hart, Zabaleta, Kompany (c), Lescott, Clichy, Y Toure (de Jong 44), Barry (Dzeko 69), Nasri, Silva, Tevez (Balotelli 76), Aguero
Goals: Zabaleta (39), Dzeko (90+2), Aguero (90+4)

On a day when nothing could possibly go wrong, it looked like something would go wrong. City, only needing to beat QPR – threatened by relegation and down to ten men – to win the league, found themselves losing as the board went up for stoppage time in the second half. They needed two goals in the five added minutes and this time it was worse than against Gillingham – back in 1999, they'd scored as the board was going up, but in 2012 they hadn't.

'We'll never see the likes of that happening again,' we had all thought as we'd celebrating that victory on penalties against Gillingham. How wrong we were – we'd see the same again, but this time on the world stage. And it would be City responsible for one of the most iconic league finishes ever. As Aguero swung his boot to bury the ball in Kenny's net, I remember thinking: 'Why didn't you go down?' knowing that Balotelli, perhaps City's best ever penalty taker, was on the pitch and seeing very clearly how the Argentine's back foot was taken in his running motion.

Thank goodness he stayed on his feet.

Yaya Toure was then immediately substituted, his importance to the team apparent. Roberto Mancini didn't want to take him off while City still needed to score, but having got in front, he felt confident that the first part of the job had been done and now they just needed to stay in front. And you couldn't blame him based on the form books that season.

But Manchester City do for the form books what the casino does for my bank balance.

Coming out for the second half, the blues had a fairly simple task: Don't concede and that would be enough to make sure they lifted the trophy for the first time in nearly four and a half decades. It took just three minutes of the second half for that plan to have made its excuses and left, leaping straight through the window without even bothering to open it first.

A high ball in the middle of the pitch looked simple to deal with. The referee, ready to give a free kick to the visitors for a late challenge on Shaun Wright-Phillips by Gael Clichy, didn't appear to be anticipating an advantage. And, when the head of Joleon Lescott met it, few in the ground expected what happened next. The centre-back, who had had an almost flawless season and formed the pairing that had been part of the best defence in the league for the previous two years, misjudged his clearance. Instead of up and away, he could only flick it on. Mike Dean signalled play on and, running on to the

Joleon Lescott

Born: 16 Aug 1982
Signed: 25 Aug 2009
Sold: -

Apps: 121 (15 sub)
Clean Sheets: 56
Goals: 9
Yellow Cards: 7
Red Cards: 0
Notes: Was sent off at Maine Road playing for Wolves for a foul on Ali Benarbia in City's 1-0 win in December 2001.

loose ball, Djibril Cisse smashed his shot first time past the onrushing Joe Hart.

But it was only a small setback. The blues hadn't exactly been at their best, but they just needed to score another to go back to the top of the league. And even with the scores level, Sunderland might have done the club a favour and bagged one against United. Right?

In theory City's task should have become easier just before the hour mark. Carlos Tevez had a bit of a dig at Joey Barton and it went unnoticed by the officials, as it was subtly done as part of the Argentine's running movements. However, about as subtle as a one-man band striding down the centre of Market Street on a Saturday afternoon was the ex-City player's response. With the assistant referee looking along the line of the 18-yard box, Barton decided his best course of action involved both his own right elbow and Tevez's left cheekbone and the midfielder took it upon himself to introduce them to each other.

If that was deemed too subtle a response still – and, let's be honest here, it wasn't the most understated of incidents already – Barton had more up his sleeve. The one-man band had suddenly become a full blown orchestra, complete with dancing elephants and fireworks, as, having been shown the red card by Mike Dean, he proceeded to knee Aguero in the back and aim a head-butt at Kompany, while his team-mates and ex-team-mate Micah Richards tried to lead him away down the tunnel.

So, playing against ten men with half an hour to score one goal that will be enough to lift the Premier League title. If anything, that challenge is just *too* easy, isn't it? This is Manchester City and they had been doing things the simple way for too long now under Roberto Mancini. It was time to throw a little spice into the bargain – six minutes after the red card, and with the home side camped in Queens Park Rangers' penalty area, the ball broke down the left flank.

As It Happened

4.19pm
Rooney scores at Sunderland to put United top of the table.

4.38pm
Zabaleta sends City back to the top of the league.

4.43pm
City lose Yaya Toure to a hamstring injury.

5.02pm
Cisse equalises for QPR and United are back in first place.

5.09pm
QPR's Barton is dismissed for violent conduct.

5.21pm
Mackie puts QPR ahead and United go three points clear.

5.47pm
Dzeko pulls the Blues level with a stoppage time header.

5.49pm
Full time at Sunderland.

5.50pm
Aguero scores with about a minute left on the clock.

5.51pm
Aguero is booked for taking his shirt off.

Traore skipped past Kompany and delivered a decent ball into the middle.

Every City fan in the ground held their breath, as Jamie Mackie arrived on cue to head into the net.

It was a strange goal for the Blues to concede and, indeed, the mood inside the stadium reflected that. Normally, when a shot beat the goalkeeper into the City net, there would be a combination of groans and sighs and grumbles. There would be the odd fan who would swear and shout to let out the frustration of going a goal down. But, on the afternoon of Sunday 13 May 2012, at around about 5.21pm, there was simply an overwhelming sense of numbness in the City crowd.

This was a day where it should have been a simple and comfortable victory, ending in City lifting the Premier League trophy. But now, with 24 minutes plus stoppage time remaining, it was a salvage job. The efforts of 37 league matches had come down to this and, when it looked like they needed to stand tall and fight, City appeared to be bottling it.

There was still enough time on the clock for a lot of fans to believe. Scoring two goals was simple, surely? It would take City's tally for that game to three – and the blues had hit three or more on 13 of their previous 18 home league matches that season. There was still a sense of hope around the ground.

But, as the QPR line dropped ever deeper and Roberto Mancini added more forward players to the pitch, the hope seeped away. The clock on the big screen got more attention than the actual action on the pitch, as fans watched while the seconds seemed to move quicker than they should have done and United edged ever closer to the finish line on the title.

Just under 13 years earlier, City had been playing a game with similar meaning resting on it, as they took on Gillingham in the Nationwide League Division Two playoff final. It was a completely different club back then, as, without promotion that year, there was the very real possibility that it might cease to exist. Needing to win, City had found themselves two goals down and it was looking like it was all over.

In the stands at Wembley that day, was the 11-year-old me. With stoppage time approaching and two goals needed, my mum put her arm around me to explain that sometimes you win and sometimes you lose.

Man City 3-2 QPR

Shots
Man City: 35
QPR: 3

Shots on Target
Man City: 24
QPR: 3

Possession
Man City: 62%
QPR: 38%

Corners
Man City: 19
QPR: 0

Today would be another of those losing occasions for City. I didn't want to know. Instead, I stood there glum and crying.

Fast forward to the final day of the 2011-12 season and, sitting next to my mum in the Etihad Stadium, we exchanged knowing glances, both of which said 'we've messed this up, haven't we?' Afterwards, she said to me that, when she looked at my 24-year-old face that day, she could only see the little boy who had been crying at Wembley. The club had changed so much since that match in 1999, but, all the while, it couldn't have been more the same. Anybody worried about the influx of money from a rich owner ruining the nature of the club clearly needn't have been.

I turned to my left. Beside me was sat a lady and her son, both of who live somewhere near me (I'm not exactly sure where, though we have bumped into each other when out and about on the streets). When I looked at his face, as he sat and watched what felt like the inevitable happen, I knew exactly what my mum saw in 1999. The sheer devastation in his eyes was horrible to see, while looking at the pitch was worse, because that meant I was directly watching my beloved club's downfall. I opted to watch the clock, but as Balotelli had a header well pushed away by Kenny, they took the clocks off the screens. And that meant only one thing: stoppage time.

> **Sergio Aguero**
>
> **Born:** 2 Jun 1988
> **Signed:** 27 Jul 2011
> **Sold:** -
>
> **Apps:** 69 (19 sub)
> **Goals:** 47
> **Yellow Cards:** 5
> **Red Cards:** 0
> **Notes:** Has a tattoo on his right arm inscribed in Tengwar – a fictional language from The Lord of the Rings.

While a lot of fans would have been willing the ball towards the Queens Park Rangers net, strangely all I could think was 'what am I going to say to the United fan in work tonight?' And I had nothing. I just couldn't come up with an excuse and I feared the mocking I was about to receive. This was going to be worse than I had ever experienced, that was for sure.

It was only when I got to work that evening when I discovered that the United fan wasn't in – he'd ("coincidentally", I might add) picked up some work starting very early on the Monday in London and, as such, couldn't be in the office that evening. Convenient isn't really the word to do the situation justice, especially when you consider the same thing happened when City beat United by six goals to one at Old Trafford.

Just like 1999, the fourth official showed five minutes. And, just like in 1999, City pulled a goal back inside the first minute of the additional time – then it was Kevin Horlock, this time it was Edin Dzeko. Though few fans will have had any sort of cognitive thought process at this time – I know all my brain was doing was thinking the line 'come on, it's just one more' over and over and over again – looking back it's difficult not to take the cynical view that the players had only done it as a cruel way of giving the supporters some more false hope.

The team of 1999 took longer to get their second goal than that of 2012, but they both scored what they needed to. Paul Dickov slotted in a neat finish into the roof of Vince Bartram's goal to earn the Blues extra time in that playoff final, while Sergio Aguero stayed on his feet under pressure to power a shot almost through Paddy Kenny. On both occasions, the roof came off the stadium.

Game 38:
Man City 3-2 QPR
Sunderland 0-1 Man Utd

		W	D	L	GD	Pts
1	Man City	28	5	5	64	89
2	Man Utd	28	5	5	56	89

I often wonder if it's part of Manchester City that, every decade or so, the club will score two important goals in stoppage time. But, in order to get that, they end up sacrificing their right to complain when other teams – usually Manchester United – score in the final seconds against them. Is there a quota of late goals each team is allowed and does the importance of the ones City have scored recently mean that we can't expect another two meaningful ones until 2025?

I'm not ashamed to say that, as both of those goals went in, the 11-year-old and the 24-year-old me hugged complete strangers more than we should have done. The sheer elation and, more than anything, relief flooded out of everybody and, from the tense 90+3 minutes that had gone before it, the 94th minute onwards was such a weight off the shoulders that it was actually tiring.

I like to think that, in those celebrations (where I picked up several mysterious bruises and ended up three rows further forward than where I had started), my mum saw the same reaction in the 24-year-old as in the 11-year-old.

The only difference would have been that, in 2012, I wasn't crying.

Definitely not.

Honest.

Seven Times When I Have Cried Over Manchester City
1. While losing 0-1 to Gillingham in 1999.
2. While losing 0-2 to Gillingham in 1999.
3. While losing 1-2 to Gillingham in 1999.
4. After a 3-1 defeat at Everton in 2001.
5. Following relegation against Ipswich in 2001.
6. After kicking the seat when Scholes scored with 17 seconds left to play in the 2010 Manchester derby.
7. When Sergio Aguero won the title for City.

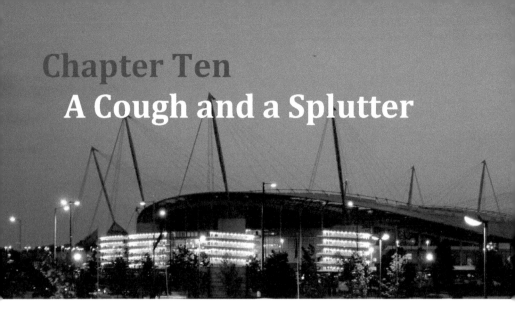

Chapter Ten
A Cough and a Splutter

IN MAY 2012, I COMPETED in the Great Manchester Run. Ridiculously underprepared and completely naïve as to the actual difficulty of running 10 kilometres on a Sunday morning, I made my way to the start line feeling totally confident in ignorance of the horror of what was waiting for me past the finish line. I had done some training, believing that I had done enough – for the weeks leading up to that morning, I'd been doing about five or six kilometres every couple of days. My advice is, simply, do more than that. Not that I ever want to put non-runners off from doing something like this, far from it. All I do want to do is prepare you correctly.

Being a man who isn't especially confident in his body shape, I was loathed to wear solely the rather thin and frankly far too revealing running vest that had been provided to me by my charity. Equally, though, I didn't want them to miss out on the publicity of having a slightly plump mid-20s bloke sweating through a crowd with their logo all over his body, so I put it on over the top of the shirt I was planning to run in – a Manchester City 2009-10 home jersey.

As the 1km sign approached, I was feeling fairly confident, still yet to properly get out of second gear. I was going strong and keeping pace with somebody slightly ahead of me because I thought they were very attractive. If that's not an incentive to run quicker, I don't know what is. Plus I kept getting overtaken by a man carrying a canoe and there's no dignity whatsoever in being a reasonably fit young lad and being beaten by someone twice his age dragging the additional weight of a boat (with leg holes cut out in the hull).

By the time we hit 4km, I was starting to regret the decision to wear the City shirt. My entire upper body was roasting, it was sticking to my back and started to feel quite heavy, which was fairly unhelpful considering the course was still heading uphill. However, just around the corner from that marker on Sunday 20 May 2012, I was treated to a selection of City fans enjoying their day, as the course took us directly past Old Trafford. I hadn't spotted the number of City shirts on display that day, but by this stage there were hundreds of badges being kissed and naughty hand gestures towards the stadium itself.

And, to be fair, you could hardly blame them. Seven days earlier, those fans had just witnessed their team win the league at their rivals' expense. Personally, I chose not to kiss the badge on my shirt. Partly because I'm a pessimist who was worried that the 2012-13 season would carry a nasty bite, but mainly because it involved lifting at least one arm from my side up to my face and I was fairly certain it would fall off if I even attempted it.

As the summer raged on, the very fact that Manchester City were once again league champions never ceased to amuse. It was a novelty, a feeling that would take many months to wear off for many supporters.

When the new season finally arrived, many fans – myself included – were looking forward to seeing the

Champions in action and seeing them hopefully go one better than the season before in one way or another. It could be success in Europe, it could be retaining the league title and winning it on points, or it could have been a cup double – either way, the fans were looking forward to a bright future.

However, the beginning to the season was somewhat muted. The Community Shield, which was seemingly taken more seriously this time than the last one the club contested, showed City for the Jekyll and Hyde outfit that they could be. Chelsea, also dangerous on the attack and with a whole new forward line to show off, took the lead just before half time. Right before the break, the London club went down to ten men and, in the space of 12 second half minutes, City ran riot.

The possession play, the movement, the vision, and the range of passing on display were all a joy to behold. In fact, the quality was better than most of what had happened throughout the title-winning campaign, and this was a positive sign for the fans. Though the fact it finished 3-2 to City and that Chelsea had the opportunity to press towards the end was less encouraging.

But still, a win's a win.

And it was pretty much the same attitude that followed the first Premier League match of the season. The visitors to the Etihad were Southampton, a newly-promoted side given the task of taking on the Champions in their own back yard. From the Saints' point of view, they had nothing to lose: they weren't expected to take anything from the game and a defeat this early in the season left them 37 games to catch up. It was hardly like a defeat would be a disaster for their survival ambitions.

City lost Sergio Aguero to injury early in the match. After that, the Blues took charge of the game and, eventually, went ahead through Carlos Tevez just before half time. The pattern of the game would reflect how the season would go as a whole – City attacked and attacked, but the ball just wouldn't go into the net. At times, some of the football was breath taking, though the final product ended up high, wide or against the woodwork.

However, two pieces of slack defending let the visitors come back to go in front. Both of the away side's goals could have been stopped, as they both contained moments when the ball could have been cleared or players could have been marked or tackles could have been stronger. Just like on the final day of the season before, a rescue job was needed and, just like on the final day of the season before, it came – this time via Dzeko and Nasri.

The fixture list hadn't been as kind to City as it had the year before. Following the home game against one of the promoted sides, the Blues had being given a run of matches where, providing they beat two old bogey teams in Tottenham and Everton, many fans were saying they could see City going unbeaten until at least the first Manchester

Comparison of Home Games

2012-13	2011-12	Points Swing
Arsenal (1-1)	Arsenal (1-0)	-2
Sunderland (3-0)	Sunderland (3-3)	+2
Everton (1-1)	Everton (2-0)	-2
Man Utd (2-3)	Man Utd (1-0)	-3
Liverpool (2-2)	Liverpool (3-0)	-2
Norwich (2-3)	Norwich (5-1)	-3

Home Points in 2011-12: 55
Home Points in 2012-13: 45

Home Goals in 2011-12: 55
Home Goals in 2012-13: 41

derby in October. As it happens, the run was longer.

This time, though, a few of the 'easier' fixtures were followed by those expecting to be challenging for Europe or pushing towards an attempt on the title.

The second match took the Blues to Anfield where, once again, it was the home side who were the better team for most of the 90 minutes. City scraped a draw, thanks to two goals from two individual errors, as Pepe Reina went on a mystery tour of his penalty area and Martin Skrtel, for reasons best known to himself, played Tevez in to round the goalkeeper.

After the home win against Queens Park Rangers – which featured more iffy defending from the Blues, this time courtesy of Aleksandar Kolarov – City made hard work of picking up points. Draws against Stoke and Arsenal featured yet more problems at the back as, in the latter, the Blues couldn't handle the pressure exerted on their

Comparison of Away Games

2012-13	2011-12	Points Swing
Fulham (1-2)	Fulham (2-2)	+2
West Brom (1-2)	West Brom (0-0)	+2
West Ham (0-0)	Wolves (0-2)	-2
Chelsea (0-0)	Chelsea (1-2)	+1
Arsenal (0-2)	Arsenal (1-0)	+3
QPR (0-0)	QPR (2-3)	-2
Soton (3-1)	Blackburn (0-4)	-3
Tottenham (3-1)	Tottenham (1-5)	-3
Swansea (0-0)	Swansea (1-0)	+1

Away Points in 2011-12: 34
Away Points in 2012-13: 33

Away Goals in 2011-12: 38
Away Goals in 2012-13: 25

defensive line for most of the second half.

The first clean sheet of the season finally arrived in October, as City took maximum points against Sunderland at home and kept the visitors blank for the afternoon. Questions about the sturdiness of the defence were being counter-questioned by the transfers from the previous summer. In this first shut-out of the campaign, it was the first occasion since the Community Shield that no new signing had been involved in the match (well, until Rodwell came on with around 90 seconds to go).

Defensive issues were beginning to plague the club and they resurfaced as the Blues made the trip to The Hawthorns. With just 23 minutes played, captain Vincent Kompany uncharacteristically gave the ball away in midfield and allowed Shane Long the chance to run at goal. Trying to cover the skipper, James Milner dived in and brought the forward down, taking none of the ball. With just the keeper to beat, it was clear what colour the card was going to be. Gone are the days when a player begins to walk before the card is shown, but the look on Milner's face told the story. He knew what Mark Clattenburg was going to do. He'd taken one for the team.

If City were getting themselves into gear for the season, it was taking a long time. They had turned the key in the ignition a long time ago, but clearly the clutch was proving problematic and the gear lever heavy to move. An

---

Roberto Mancini Defensive Record

PL Goals Conceded
09-10: 16 (21 games)
10-11: 33 (38 games)*
11-12: 29 (38 games)*
12-13: 31 (36 games)*

PL Clean Sheets
09-10: 7 (21 games)
10-11: 18 (38 games)*
11-12: 17 (38 games)
12-13: 17 (36 games)*

*Best in the league

unconvincing win over Swansea was followed by a goalless draw at West Ham, in a game the Blues should have been winning to keep up their title aspirations. Nevertheless, after a late comeback against Tottenham and a rout against Aston Villa, City were finally back on top of the table.

It was over, though, as soon as it started. After City's 0-0 draw at Chelsea, the Blues never made the summit of the table again all season. Their time on top of the pile during their title defence lasted just seven days.

By the time the first Manchester derby of the year arrived, the situation was remarkably similar to the season before: City were three points behind their rivals, the Blues had a better goal difference and a win would take them back to the top of the table. But a lot had changed since April. United were full of confidence and picking up points they didn't deserve. City were defending poorly for spells and throwing away leads.

This time around, United won. It was a last minute deflected free kick from Robin van Persie, a player who undoubtedly played a huge role in the Reds reaching top spot and a player who Roberto Mancini had wanted, but missed out on. And that goal had given United a six point buffer.

The Christmas period didn't treat City too badly, as only one game didn't end in victory. It was the traditional 1-0 defeat at Sunderland. That, however, wasn't good enough, as the Christmas period treated United better. By the turn of the New Year, the gap was up to seven points.

January worked out the same for both City and United – with three wins and a draw from the four Premier League games. But it was impossible to help feeling like City had missed an opportunity. United hadn't been bleeding too many points since August and after their draw against Tottenham on Sunday 20 January 2013, the gap was back down to five points as City had beaten Fulham the day

Southampton 3-1 Manchester City
Saturday 9 February 2013, Premier League

City: Hart, Zabaleta, Garcia, Lescott (Kolarov 66), Clichy, Y Toure (c), Barry, Nasri (Milner 55), Silva (Maicon 73), Aguero, Dzeko
Goals: Dzeko (39)

Sometimes players have bad games and there's very little that can be done about it. Whatever they try just doesn't work, they control the ball as far as they can kick it and they slip when through on goal, with a great chance to score. However, that's often just one player in the team.

What happens when that's eleven members of the squad? Well, Southampton 3-1 Manchester City is what happens – as the hosts played the Champions off the park. In truth, it could have been more than three had the Saints taken their chances. However, it also shouldn't have been three, as all of the home side's goals were handed to them on a plate.

Barry gave the ball away for Puncheon to score, before Hart dropped a ball through his own legs allowing Davies to slide it into the unguarded goal. The third was the icing on the cake: Gareth Barry finishing into the bottom corner with a routine passback.

City never got out of neutral, let alone into first gear.

before. But it was quickly re-opened, as a toothless City side drew 0-0 at Loftus Road. It was all the incentive United needed to beat Southampton the next night.

And it was at the start of February that saw City's Premier League implosion, as the season began to collapse in on itself. Performances hadn't been brilliant for a while and, though defensively City had improved massively, the Blues were struggling to convert chances into goals. Shots were, more often than not, weakly hit, badly aimed or from 35 yards, where the goalkeeper would swallow them up with ease.

It started as Liverpool came to the Etihad and were the better side. Daniel Sturridge joined the increasingly less exclusive club of ex-players who had scored for and against City at Eastlands, and it was only a wonder goal from Sergio Aguero that earned the Blues a point – once again after Pepe Reina had decided upon a little excursion from his goalmouth.

If falling nine points behind on their title challenge with those two draws was bad, what City did next was more or less a catastrophe and almost certainly the final nail in the coffin of the championship defence. The club put in its worst performance of the season and played possibly the worst game they had since Roberto Mancini took charge. It happened on the south coast, as Southampton bettered the Blues by three goals to one. It was an awful day made worse by the knowledge that each of the Saints' goals was easily preventable, as Gareth Barry made two horrendous errors, either side of Joe Hart's Massimo Taibi impression against the same opponents.

It would take an almighty swing of 12 points for the Blues to climb above United. If City won all of their remaining fixtures, the only way they could become Champions was if United lost at least four games. By that stage, they had only dropped points in five games at all, with two of those five being draws.

A defeat at Goodison Park in mid-March started the title challenge coffin on the conveyor belt towards the incinerator, as the gap increased to 15 points. Two games later, a win in the Manchester derby at Old Trafford simply delayed the inevitable. It featured a goal of the season contender from Sergio Aguero, but it did feel somewhat flat, given it took just two more weeks for the crown to be placed on United heads.

Calling City's title defence a whimper would have been generous.

The problem for Roberto Mancini, though, was that the side hadn't performed too much better in the other competitions, barring one – the FA Cup. The draw had been kind to the Blues, given that the only Premier League side the club faced up to the semi final stage was Stoke, albeit away from home.

Having dispatched Watford in the third round, a trip to The Potteries wasn't eagerly awaited by the fans. There were many more places they'd have preferred to go, given City's dreadful record at the Britannia. Against what most expected, though, the Blues dominated and a goal from Zabaleta was enough to ensure safe passage to the fifth round and a tie with Leeds.

That turned out to be another comfortable game – where I should have been sitting next to a Leeds fan friend of mine, but he got too drunk the night before and was too hungover to make the journey over. Instead, I gave the ticket to a Bradford-supporting friend of mine, who

---

Stoke City 0-1 Manchester City
Saturday 26 January 2013
FA Cup Fourth Round

City: Pantilimon, Zabaleta, Kompany (c) (Clichy 40), Lescott, Kolarov (Aguero 62), Milner, Barry, Garcia, Silva, Dzeko, Tevez (Rodwell 86)
Goals: Zabaleta (85)

City don't do wins at Stoke. Not since Gerard Wiekens volleyed home in a 1-0 win at the Britannia Stadium in 1999 have the Blues come away from the Potteries victorious and they'd been six times before this FA Cup match. So, before kick off, many fans were hoping for a replay at best.

As thoughts turned towards a replay, Pablo Zabaleta won the ball in his own half and took a chace – laying it off in the middle and making a run down the right. It bounced to him in the Stoke box and, with five minutes to play, he put the visitors in front. It was enough to win the game.

was all too delighted to watch their rivals have a new bellybutton torn. The game was comfortable enough for us to play 'Wall or Over' whenever a free kick was given (the rules are fairly simple: in the time between the taker running at the dead ball and him kicking it, you have to decide between you whether you think the ball will hit the wall or go over the bar – whoever predicts the most correctly by full time wins).

With some big names hanging around in the hat for the sixth round, City were handed yet another favourable draw. Championship strugglers Barnsley would make the trip to the Etihad and City would go on to dispatch them with relative ease, thanks in no small part to a Carlos Tevez hat trick.

Given the draws had been so favourable and that, having been pulled out of the weird fishbowl thing on ITV at the same time as the ball corresponding to Chelsea or Manchester United for the semi final, City fans were beginning to wonder if it would be their year again. They had faced little in the way of opposition and now a win in a one-off game against a top Premier League side would give them an excellent chance of lifting silverware in a largely disappointing season.

Pablo Zabaleta

Born: 16 Jan 1985
Signed: 31 Aug 2008
Sold: -

Apps: 168 (27 sub)
Clean Sheets: 76
Goals: 7
Yellow Cards: 42
Red Cards: 4
Notes: Scored his only goal of 2011-12 in the final game of the season win over QPR.

However, with the league form being much poorer than the year before, questions began to surface about whether Roberto Mancini's job rested upon it.

A brilliant first half performance and a stubborn second half saw City do enough to get past Chelsea and into the final, where Wigan waited. Even the most cynical fans had dared to believe their name was on the cup, with a fair number of us suggesting that the winner of the City-Chelsea tie would lift the cup.

It was a dangerous line of thinking, as it turned out to be completely wrong. City just didn't turn up and Wigan fully deserved their cup victory. For whatever reason, be it the style of play, the belief that they only needed to turn up to win, or the speculation about the manager's future – on which rumours had spread like wildfire the night before that he would lose his job come what may – the team just didn't play as a team.

In a period of the club's history where trophies were being lifted or Champions League qualification chased, it felt odd that the game with Reading after the cup final defeat was the first of two damp squib matches. It didn't matter what City did.

It would also turn out to be the first game the club would play in the post-Mancini era, as, a year to the day after he lifted the Premier League title for the club, the Italian was relieved of his duties.

How times change.

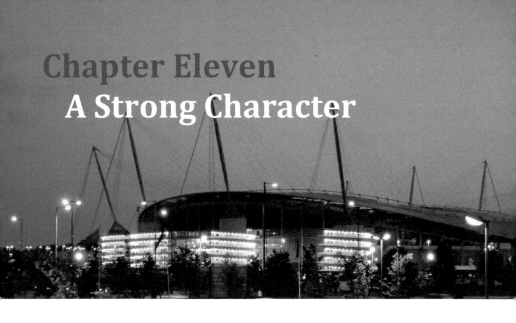

Chapter Eleven
A Strong Character

PUNDITS AND EX-PROFESSIONALS THAT ADORN various television studios across the country often say that it takes a certain type of player to become a manager. In fact, the phrases "I always knew he would go into management" or "he always seemed the type to be interested in coaching" always seem to easily roll off the tongue of those who were more the type to put on a suit and tie and talk about the national sport in front of a room full of cameras. It should be pointed out, I'm not knocking that career option, some players are a natural at it and others are... well... less so.

Looking back over his career, Roberto Mancini is someone who was definitely cut out for management. He is strong willed and sticks to his principles, no matter how much the watching millions think or want him to change. This isn't necessarily a good thing, given how his time with City ended, but it's vital in having the right character to take up the job. With the Blues, he was always bold enough to try something and, if it didn't work, then he'd try to dissect it and make it work.

He was also known to have taken half time team talks

when captain of Sampdoria, which is probably one of the biggest clues that he was cut out to be in the dugout when he playing days were over.

In fact, it's interesting to look back at his time as a player and how that influenced his style of management. Unquestionably, Mancini liked to work on the edge when in the dugout. It seemed the chances of there being a heated exchange of words between himself and another were always high, but that's not necessarily a bad form of motivation.

As a child, football was high up on his list of priorities and it suddenly becomes clear why he never took to the showbiz lifestyles that some players in the modern game lead. He even advised his players at City that "it is better to go with a woman" after a match than going out for a drink.

Soon after his son took charge of City, Mancini's father Aldo explained to *The Sun* about the two biggest parts of Roberto's childhood: religion and football. He explained that the only time the Italian didn't have a football with him was when he was carrying out altar boy duties and that, on the day of his first Holy Communion, an eight-year old Mancini was upset at having to miss a match with his team to go to church. Having taken Communion, the priest – who ran the team when he could – told Roberto to sneak out and change into his kit, having heard the team were 2-0 down. They didn't lose.

When older and having proved to be one of the best strikers in Italy during his 15 years at Sampdoria, Mancini judged it to be his responsibility to always be better. He had been given a talent that few others had, so it was down to him to make sure that the team won. When they needed somebody to stand up and be counted, he felt like it was he himself that should shoulder the responsibility. He had the ability, so he had work harder to use it to support those who couldn't meet his standards.

Suddenly, his post-match comments about his own players don't seem so surprising. The standard answer for a manager to give when asked about a player who's just had a good game is to agree with the interviewer and sing the player's praises. Not Mancini.

No, Mancini preferred to confirm that his man had played well and add they he was a good player – let's be honest, at Mancini's City, they were all good players and they wouldn't be at the club if they weren't. But then he would finish his answer with the often seemingly harsh statement that "he must improve". Or, when the team had played well and won, he'd say, "we must continue to improve".

And it was all part of his own personal standards. The players performing well deserved praise for their displays, but they also need to work harder to help the team, just like Roberto Mancini the player.

When asked on Italian TV to describe himself in one word, Roberto Mancini plumped for "genius". There is his personality in a nutshell – cheeky, but with a self-confidence and belief in his own ability. His fiery, confrontational attitude has always been with him and he's never been someone afraid of backing himself and sticking to his guns. As a teenager in his first season at Sampdoria, he was involved in a training ground bust-up with his teammate Trevor Francis in a practice match. It continued into the dressing room afterwards and the pair needed to be separated to avoid a full blown scrap.

If there were to be any clue about Mancini's managerial temperament from his playing days, it would be while he was Sven Goran Eriksson's captain. In a match against Inter Milan in 1995, the Italian blew a fuse when he was denied a penalty in the opening stages of the game, telling the referee exactly what he thought of the decision. He tore off his captain's armband and stormed from the pitch, telling his manager that he was never going to play again. Having been persuaded to return, Mancini was then sent off for a lunge at Paul Ince after just 34 minutes.

Suddenly, Mancini's handling of Mario Balotelli doesn't seem so odd. Numerous managers would have been quick to move the number 45 on following an ever-growing list of misdemeanours, but not Mancini. Maybe the manager saw something of himself in the striker, whose full potential was never really realised in a City shirt. Maybe that upset Mancini because it fell short of what he expected of himself and, later, his players. And Mancini's seemingly never-ending "oh, Mario, I can't stay mad at you" attitude becomes clear and, equally, it's obvious why Balotelli saw his manager as more of a father figure – it's like they're the same person, one generation on.

Over Mancini's City career, there were more than a couple of mirrors towards his time as a player. Despite being a rising talent, his international career was something of a damp squid. In fact, he only featured in one major tournament for his country – the 1988 European Championships, in which he opened the scoring – winning just 36 caps and scoring four goals.

In a time when Italy were one of the world's footballing super-powers, he was always facing great competition for the striking roles, but with the added problem of having got off on the wrong foot with the manager. Having made his international debut against Canada in a 1984 tour of North America, he played the next game against the USA in New York. After that match, the impressionable 19-year-old Mancini was invited out into the city by Marco Tardelli and Claudio Gentile to celebrate. He broke curfew and, on returning to the team's hotel, found his manager Enzo Bearzot waiting for him.

They rowed and, unsurprisingly, Mancini defended his corner. The next morning, having slept on the incident, the striker stuck to his guns and found himself embroiled in another argument with his boss. The result was a promise from Bearzot that the striker would never represent the national team again while he was in charge and he was true to his word, despite Mancini's form in Serie A.

Think back to the evening of 27 September 2011. Manchester City, losing 2-0 at Bayern Munich, were desperately trying to get back into the game. In the dugout, Mancini made his first move, swapping Edin Dzeko for Nigel de Jong after 54 minutes, in an attempt to get the visitors more possession – since the opening quarter of an

---

Bayern Munich 2-0 Manchester City
Tuesday 27 September 2011, Champions League Group A

City: Hart, Richards, Kompany (c), K Toure, Clichy, Y Toure, Barry (Kolarov 73), Nasri (Milner 69), Aguero, Silva, Dzeko (de Jong 55)
Goals: -

The 90 minutes of football played at Allianz Arena will be a minor footnote in what happened on the night Bayern Munich beat Manchester City in their first Champions League away game. Instead, what most fans will remember from this autumnal evening was the Mancini-Tevez bust up.

The striker, having warmed up for large parts of the second half, had been asked by the manager to continue doing so, in order to prepare him to join the action. However, believing that he had stretched as much as he needed to, Tevez refused and on the bench there was a row.

Mancini declined to bring the forward on, chossing Milner and Kolarov as the attacking options instead. With constant rumours from the year before about Tevez's desire to leave the club, it seemed that it was the end of the line for the forward, especially after Roberto Mancini's post match comments.

It resulted in a five month exile for the striker and an internal disciplinary action from the club.

---

hour, the Blues had barely controlled the play and the strikers had become isolated.

The plan, as the manager explained after the match, was to get the team back into the game and get them seeing more of the ball, and then to throw Carlos Tevez into the mix. But there was a row between Mancini and the Argentine, as the manager instructed him to warm up ready for his introduction and the striker refused, believing himself to have done enough preparations. It didn't go down well and both parties fought their corner.

After the match, Mancini immediately told the press that Tevez would never play for City again while he was the manager and that he couldn't accept the striker's behaviour. Later, however, that position was revised, with the manager insisting that Tevez – who had taken a period of self-imposed exile back in Argentina – would be welcome back at City, providing he was willing to apologise.

The similarities with Mancini's own actions in New York are striking. Had he chosen to apologise to Bearzot and admit he was in the wrong rather than stand his ground, especially the morning after, his international career could have hit the heights his talent probably deserved. Having learnt from that experience and despite having promised Tevez would never feature in one of his City teams again, Mancini offered the hand of reconciliation, perhaps out of regret of what had happened to him.

The following February, Tevez returned from exile and issued an unreserved apology. He then returned to action as a substitute against Chelsea in March, making his first start since the incident in Munich in early April in a 4-0 win over West Brom. City won the remainder of the games that season, in which Tevez started all six.

The echoes between how Mancini handled his time in charge of City and his own playing career are clear. He learnt many lessons through his life and, despite remaining a fierce character and strong willed, he was able to see where he had gone wrong in the past and correct it (or try to) later in his career when similar events occurred.

However, perhaps his biggest fault was his inability to change his philosophies when it came to his players and the media. It was reported Mancini didn't read the English papers and, as such, cared little about what they wrote, which could have been part of the problem. It was also suggested that he didn't like to lie, meaning he spoke freely and was fairly liberal with his opinions.

Meanwhile, there were frequent reports that his players were often unhappy with what they were reading when the news pages were delivered of a morning. And perhaps this is the one lesson that Mancini didn't learn quickly enough.

In terms of his playing ability and his managerial knowledge, maybe Mancini was right to describe himself as a "genius" in that TV interview. However, if that is the case, like most described as such, he had his faults, which occasionally outweighed his positives. Never have the words 'flawed genius' been more appropriate.

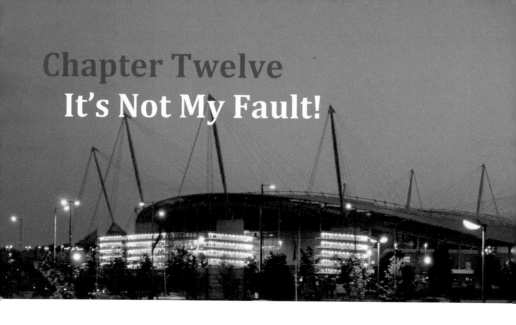

Chapter Twelve
It's Not My Fault!

I F THERE'S ANYTHING THAT *The Empire Strikes Back* taught us, then it's this: whatever problem it is you're facing, whether something isn't working or has broken down entirely (especially the hyperspace generator), the best course of action is to hit something and shout at the top of your voice the words "It's not my fault!"

On the Manchester City bench, the role of the metal plating over the door panel on the *Millennium Falcon* was so often played by Brian Kidd's arm. Every time a City attack broke down or one of the players did something that Roberto Mancini wasn't especially happy with, the Italian would channel his inner Han Solo and beat seven bells out of the arm of the man sitting next to him. And then offer him a Fruit Pastille.

However, there is a point to me bringing up the best *Star Wars* film at the start of this chapter. As the team struggled through the 2012-13 season, the phrase 'It's not my fault!' was never actually uttered by anybody on the management team, but there were a few occasions when it felt like the fans were being given excuse after excuse as to why the Blues defended their title so badly. After all, a case could be made for City having the strongest squad in the league, but they certainly didn't have the strongest team. The whole was certainly not any greater than the sum of the parts.

It started before the season, as Roberto Mancini seemingly struggled to bring in additional players. As the summer months wore on and other teams began to dabble in the transfer market, City were surprisingly quiet. For a club that had financial clout, yet not without caution given the financial fair play rulings that would soon be coming in, City seemed fairly calm about the situation.

As with summer 2011, both City and title rivals United were in the market for the same player. They year before it had been Arsenal's Samir Nasri, with the Frenchman choosing City at the eleventh hour. However, one year on, City's pursuit of Robin van Persie looked somewhat more laid back – for Nasri, the club went all guns blazing, while for the Dutchman they appeared to be playing it slow.

Summer 2012 Transfers

Players In
Jack Rodwell (£12m)
Scott Sinclair (£8m)
Maicon (undisclosed)
Richard Wright (free)
Matija Nastasic (part-ex)
Javi Garcia (£16m)

Players Out
Emmanuel Adebayor (£5m)
Vladimir Weiss (undisclosed)
Greg Cunningham (free)
Owen Hargreaves (released)
Gunnar Nielsen (released)
Stuart Taylor (free)
Adam Johnson (£10m)
Nigel de Jong (undisclosed)
Stefan Savic (part-ex)

Arsene Wenger didn't want to sell him, that was for certain. And it wasn't just that he'd been Arsenal's talisman for 2011-12, but also the nature of the two clubs involved. There had been talk of Juventus expressing an interest, but that never really materialised. This was a duel between

Manchester and London, and reports suggested Wenger was keen not to let him join the Blues, having lost four players in that direction in recent years.

Equally, he wasn't overjoyed at the idea of selling to United, but sometimes an offer is too good to refuse, especially for a player who could soon leave for nothing as he was nearing the end of his contract.

By the time the signing was made and van Persie was announced as a United player, City were well off the pace. It looked like their slow game had been far too lethargic and they missed out on one of the players who would turn out to be a key factor in the Premier League title returning to Old Trafford. All season, City's problem was converting chances into goals. All season, van Persie netted for United.

2011-12
Sergio Aguero: 30 goals (48 apps)
Mario Balotelli: 17 goals (32 apps)
Edin Dzeko: 19 goals (43 apps)
Carlos Tevez: 4 goals (15 apps)

Robin van Persie: 37 goals (48 apps)

2012-13
Sergio Aguero: 17 goals (40 apps)
Mario Balotelli: 3 goals (20 apps)
Edin Dzeko: 15 goals (45 apps)
Carlos Tevez: 17 goals (47 apps)

Robin van Persie: 30 goals (48 apps)

Another of Mancini's big targets for the summer, Daniele de Rossi, was missed, too. This one seemed to be a much more straightforward battle between two clubs – Roma, where the player was contracted to, and City, who wanted to buy him. City were again dragging their heels and refusing to up their valuation of the midfielder, while Roma were refusing to budge on their asking price. In the end, a press conference was called where the Italian announced he'd be staying in Italy. It was an announcement many had seen coming, because he was hardly going to walk into the press room at the Stadio Olimpico and reveal he was leaving.

City didn't confirm their first signing until the morning of the Community Shield – seven days before their first Premier League fixture of the new campaign. Mancini often spoke about players getting a full pre-season, so it seemed odd that he would intentionally wait until this late in the transfer window to make any moves in the market. And when he did, it wasn't for a player that many fans saw as on the radar, with Jack Rodwell joining from Everton.

With fans expecting more as the season quickly approached, they were sorely disappointed, with Rodwell remaining the only inbound player for the first match of the season.

Following a draw at Liverpool the week after, there had still been no movement. When asked about the situation with bringing players in, Mancini had often responded that the club were working on it, but it was a question that needed to be put towards the Football Administration Officer, Brian Marwood. He cut a frustrated figure as, for his third post-match press conference of the season and the second in the Premier League, he was talking about players who the club were yet to bring in. And while he insisted there was no problem between himself and Marwood, the inference that he was frustrated by the lack of transfer activity spoke louder and suggested that he was, in fact, piling pressure on the man in charge of the chequebook to get some players in. It seemed like Mancini was willing to risk cutting off his own scarf to spite his dress sense, as he pushed against Marwood and Marwood pushed back.

It took until transfer deadline day for more players to arrive. The first was Richard Wright, in a move that the football world reacted to with an 'I didn't realise he was still around', before Scott Sinclair joined in a deal that many assumed was about filling the now-departed Adam

Johnson's role. Maicon was next through the door, followed by Matija Nastasic. As the clock ticked down towards midnight, one more name was added to the squad – Javi Garcia.

Without knowing how quickly the Serbian centre-back was going to turn out to be a first team player, the list was still seemingly lacking that marquee signing. Wright was clearly a option to replace Stuart Taylor as third choice goalkeeper, while Sinclair was likely going to be a fringe player at most, with players like Nasri or Silva occupying what would probably be his role in the team. Maicon, at 31, wasn't getting any younger and was seemingly brought in to be the right-sided Kolarov in a 3-5-2 system. Nastasic was one for the future, while Garcia promised big things thanks to his performances at Benfica.

As the window closed and City fans reflected on the business, it was difficult to see whether the squad had improved from the year before. The players that had come in felt like they weren't the club's first choices and, as the season progressed, it became apparent that it had been a poor summer for the Blues. For whatever reason, be it injuries or a lack of first team chances or problems settling in England, it looked like only one of the signings had been a huge success, as Matija Nastasic knocked a very experienced and reliable defender in Joleon Lescott out of the team.

While it might have been Marwood's slow deals that had meant the club missed out on first choice players, Mancini's public criticisms were ill-advised. It seemed the

Matija Nastasic

Born: 28 Mar 1993
Signed: 31 Aug 2012
Sold: -

Apps: 30 (0 sub)
Clean Sheets: 12
Goals: 0
Yellow Cards: 2
Red Cards: 0
Notes: Made his debut against Real Madrd in the Bernabeu.

more the manager expressed his frustration about business not being completed quickly, the more the football administrator became adamant that the Blues wouldn't be taken for a ride financially. And this resulted in a mad panic on the last day of the window to get some new faces through the door.

Getting off to such an unhelpful start hindered league progress somewhat and performances weren't up there with the classic matches being produced in the season before. To try and combat the problems he had

Wing Backs and Three Central Defenders

Throughout the 2011-12 season, despite City winning the title, they often found breaking down opposition defences to be quite tough, especially away from home. One solution had been to add more width to the team's play, but it's difficult to do that without sacrificing some of the possession play to add the more natural wide players, which would lose a big part of City's game.

Over the summer, Roberto Mancini's solution became clear: the width would come from the full-backs, whose focus on defending wouldn't be as intensive as the year before. A back three, with two wing-backs, meant there would be a lot of space in the full-back positions, but the extra central defender can come across to cover while the other wing back drops in to cover on the side of the pitch not being attacked.

That meant the full-backs could act as wingers, with only a few defensive responsibilities. It also allowed Mancini to keep his two holding midfielders and two strikers, only having to sacrifice one of his attacking midfielders. In essence, there's nothing wrong with the formation, though the personnel City had to hand for the 2012-13 season meant the set-up never really stood up to scrutiny.

The theory behind the system was fine, but the execution left a lot to be desired.

encountered with his 4-2-3-1 and 4-2-2-2 formations – inverting the wingers provided plenty of ball possession, but little width and, on occasion, City could look like they would be able to play for hours and not score – Mancini tried 3-5-2. Well, 3-4-1-2 to be more specific.

The thinking behind the switch was sound and even the theory of it held plenty of water. Three central defenders would provide the cover, especially with two holding midfielders in front of them, while the full backs could be both protection on the flanks and the width further up field. It even meant Aleksandar Kolarov could focus a little less on the defensive side of his position and spend more time getting those wickedly angled and powerful balls that he excels at into the box.

However, it just didn't work.

It was a formation that left the Blues horribly exposed at the back, with few of the defenders seemingly comfortable in position. Ball retention was at an all-time minimum, as players didn't seem to know where they should be and struggled to read where their teammates would be running. Worst of all, though, it seemed Mancini didn't have the correct players to execute the formation fully – perhaps one of the biggest reasons the summer transfer policy had failed.

Gael Clichy, a natural left-back, was frequently deployed at centre-back. Pablo Zabaleta often made the same switch, though having played in midfield, the right-back seemed more comfortable than his opposite number. James Milner was often played at right full-back, while Samir Nasri had featured as a holding midfielder. It was disjointed and clumsy, but still Mancini persisted with it.

The formation itself wasn't the problem, but the lack of suitable players. It was clear this was where the signing of Maicon had come in, and it is here where it seems that missing out on de Rossi was crucial, as the Roma man's versatility would have allowed the switch from a back four to a back three without the need of making a substitution.

The away match at Ajax was the perfect example of how much of a disaster the shape was for City. Needing a win to retain any real hopes of qualifying for the next stage of the competition, Mancini switched to a back three in reaction to falling behind. From being fairly evenly matched with, if less clinical than, the Dutch club up to that point, the away side lost any grip they had on the match. A third goal was conceded and the impetus had drained away completely.

That's not to say the shape always failed, because it didn't. In fact, it won the game for City against Tottenham at the Etihad, when Maicon was introduced to provide fizzing balls in from the right. The switch earned City control of the game and Edin Dzeko snatched a late winner.

As the season wore on, City drifted back to their style of play from the year before. But the results didn't really follow and the manager found himself under increasing pressure. Following poor performances, he seemed to lash out at his team, with Joe Hart, Vincent Kompany, Samir Nasri and Mario Balotelli all coming in for public criticism over the course of 2012-13. Throughout Mancini's time with City, that list grows longer.

While an unusual method of management, public criticism does little for the players in question. Mancini will point to the fact that most of his dressing downs resulted in an upturn in the player's form as the reason why it worked, but management by confrontation can only go so far. It gets to a point where players begin to feel alienated and victimised and, no matter how justified the criticism is, the public nature of the comments will make them feel undermined. If the criticism needs to be made, it's most likely to work privately – what's said to the press should do nothing to damage any delicate egos.

Joe Hart was publicly criticised for his form, something

that he himself agreed with in one TV interview. However, it's one thing to tell the watching public that your own performances have been below the standards you set for yourself and another to have the manager do it for you.

Vincent Kompany, who had spent roughly three months injured during the season, made his comeback for the Belgian national team – a decision that upset Mancini. Speaking after the incident, the manager explained why he felt Kompany had made a mistake and, following the Belgian's substitution in the next match, the captain completely ignored the Italian in the technical area. One newspaper report suggested the two had not been on good terms since the start of the season, though it does have to be treated with some degree of scepticism.

Samir Nasri will have opened his newspaper to read that his manager would like to punch him, another ill-advised comment from the boss. The Frenchman's form did pick up, but the player hit back in an interview where he said he felt his former coach Arsene Wenger was the best he'd played under.

Perhaps the biggest sign of division between manager and players was in the shape of Mario Balotelli. A training ground bust-up was caught on camera, as it seemed like the two Italians were close to coming to blows over an incident involving a challenge on Scott Sinclair. Balotelli had been given chance after chance, after various stunts and misdemeanours throughout his City career, but this was seemingly the straw that broke the camel's back and the club sold him in January. There had always been the danger that something like that could boil over, especially give Mancini's management style.

And, even as an outsider looking in, it could be easy to think Mancini had given Balotelli more chances at City than perhaps he would have given others in that situation.

Since Mancini's sacking, newspaper reports have

suggested there were few players in the dressing room who would have been sorry to see him leave the club. Again it's impossible to take what was printed as the gospel truth, but it's understandable how that conclusion can be reached – as one report in the *Daily Mail* suggested that, following the FA Cup final defeat to Wigan, one of City's players texted a journalist to ask if the champagne could be put on ice, as rumours of the Italian's impending departure gained momentum. That same report also claimed another player had joked that 'it was a shame we have a game against Reading on Tuesday... we could have gone out to celebrate.'

And, as the *Daily Mail* pointed out, it's telling that these players had been led to an FA Cup win and a Premier League title under Mancini over the previous two seasons.

It's not a manager's job to be liked, however. Providing they get the best out of their team, there's no right or wrong way to motivate players. As soon as those motivation techniques stop having the desired effect, though, there can be trouble and that's exactly how the 2012-13 season worked for Mancini. Players would be willing to put up with his public confrontations while the team was winning, but as soon as a points gap at the top had opened up and the team's form nosedived, it bred a mood where few were willing to fight for their manager. That's not to say they didn't give their best for the team in games that didn't go City's way, but simply that a manager without a working relationship with his players can't motivate them.

In the end, when the times were getting tough, Mancini had too few allies at City. Having pointed the finger publicly at those in charge of bringing in players, at the players themselves and, on occasion, at his own backroom staff, he seemingly had nowhere to hide when the pressure was stoked up. When the going got tough and the club needed to pull together to overcome the downturn in fortunes, Mancini had burned too many bridges and there were few left to fight his corner with him.

After what would turn out to be his final game with the club, Mancini took on a new target publicly: the press office. Annoyed that rumours about his future had been leaked to the media the night before the FA Cup final, he hit out at the club's chief communications officer Vicky Kloss for not quashing the stories.

And, while there were definitely mitigating circumstances for City's poor season on the pitch, Mancini didn't help himself being stubbornly set in his ways. Whatever the outcome, the buck always has to stop with the manager.

Roberto Mancini's Post-Match Interview (Abridged)
In a small room inside Wembley, Roberto Mancini spoke to the press following City's 1-0 defeat to Wigan in the FA Cup Final.

Journalist: "You said you don't understand why the club haven't stopped the reports?"

Roberto Mancini: "Vicky or the other people who work for the press don't stop this rubbish. You have written this for six months and in the last two weeks, it's been too much. I don't understand why. For football, I answer. For the press, you should talk to Vicky and the other people. If it's true, it will be true. But for me, no. I'm happy to work for Manchester City. I'm happy with my job, about what we did in three years. I'm disappointed now because we lost this game."

Journalist: "Do you think the club should tell you if you have a future at City?"

Roberto Mancini: "They don't need to talk to me about the future. When you have a four-year contract, it's true that every contract can be broken. But I don't think they need to talk to me."

Journalist: "But it would be ridiculous to sack you, wouldn't it?"

Roberto Mancini: "In football, everything can happen. I was sacked after seven trophies with Inter."

Journalist: "There were the same reports at Inter, weren't there?"

Roberto Mancini: "Football is easy for the people who stay outside. It's easy to talk on the outside. Now, we are talking about one situation, which for me is not true."

Journalist: "Why haven't you asked anyone at City to stop these stories?"

Roberto Mancini: "Because it's not my job. I'm used to seeing these things in football."

Journalist: "These stories don't help though, do they?"

Roberto Mancini: "But I'm strong enough. I don't need anyone to help me."

Journalist: "Do you think City are a better club than Chelsea when it comes to sticking with a manager?"

Roberto Mancini: "City, for me, is a serious club. The people that are in charge at Manchester City, like Khaldoon, are fantastic men. But this problem has come out because we didn't stop all these things that you wrote for six months."

Journalist: "You said Vicky should stop these rumours but she can only do that if someone on the board tells her to?"

Roberto Mancini: "Vicky is in charge, ask her. It's difficult for me to say. I say to you one thing. When I worked for Inter Milan, for a month the newspapers wrote the same as you. I thought always, it's not true, it's not true, because we are winning. But after the Italian Cup final, I read a newspaper which is very close with Inter. One journalist wrote that Inter probably would sack me. In that moment I realised maybe it was true. I don't know whether it's true or not."

Journalist: "Arsene Wenger hasn't won a trophy for eight years, David Moyes has never won a trophy. Why are you in this situation?"

Roberto Mancini: "I don't know. We need to work hard as a squad because when you start to win trophies, maybe you can think 'we are the best team'. But it's not true because you need to work harder and harder. If the people who work with us around the team are not strong enough for this job, they should improve. I'm strong. But together, I think we should improve."

Journlaist: "Who are these people who aren't stong enough?"

Roberto Mancini: "The people, Vicky, the people that..."

Journalist: "But you can't blame Vicky?"

Roberto Mancini: "I can't stop the things that you write every day in the newspaper. For me, I don't read the newspapers. But people say to me 'are they sacking you?' I don't know if it's true."

Journalist: "You say you don't think it's true but no-one has stopped it?"

Roberto Mancini: "I think that you have written a lot of stupid things for six months. This is my opinion."

Journalist: "You're still popular with the fans, do you think that will help you keep your job?"

Roberto Mancini: "This is normal because we won. I don't think there will ever be another manager who will win 6-1 at Old Trafford against Ferguson. I was the first manager who, after 30 years, took the banner from Old Trafford. We won one Premier League, we won one FA Cup, one Charity Shield. For this reason, I am very popular with the supporters. I love them, they love me. I am very happy for this. If I leave the club, I will be the first supporter of Manchester City in the future. Now, I can say nothing. I don't know whether it's true or not."

Chapter Thirteen
Thanks for the Memories

I**T SHOULDN'T BE UNDERSTATED HOW** much good work Roberto Mancini did at Manchester City. While the previous chapter pointed out some negatives in his three and a half years with the club, it shouldn't be forgotten that he turned a City team that was proving to be a near miss on the pitch into one that was capable of winning trophies. While it turned out that his management style didn't appear to be compatible with what the board had wanted for the club, he did provide the fans with some of the best times they had seen in a long time – and for a lot of them, it was the best time they had ever had.

In fact, when it comes to Mancini losing his job, there's a good case for arguing that what happened on the pitch had very little influence. The Blues had improved every season under the Italian until his last year in charge. Even in that final year, Mancini reached a cup final and earned City's second highest ever Premier League finish.

During his time with the club, Mancini masterminded some fantastic victories, along with brilliant performances. The fans will always look back fondly over some memorable games – many of which came in the title winning 2011-12 season – where the Blues systematically picked their opponents apart. Tottenham underestimated what City could do and ended up being on the wrong end of a 5-1 battering at White Hart Lane. Edin Dzeko put in perhaps his best performance for the club and scored four of them.

Later in that season, with City two points ahead of United, the Blues had to travel to Old Trafford, where Mancini not only oversaw a great tactical victory, but it was United's heaviest ever home defeat in the Premier League. Not just that, but with City having scored three, he brought on Edin Dzeko, who was without a goal in eight games, sensing the reds were dead on their feet and the Blues could run riot. They did and Dzeko bagged two, albeit one with his knee and one straight through the goalkeeper.

Silverware

FA Cup 2011
Man City 1-0 Stoke

Premier League 2012
Man City, 89pts, +64GD

Community Shield 2012
Chelsea 2-3 Man City

This derby win was just six months on from the last competitive match between the two sides, when they met at Wembley in the FA Cup semi final. In the week before it, City had lost their star striker in Tevez to injury, while United had lost Rooney to suspension. The questions before the game were over which team would cope with their loss the better; United had scored more goals from other areas of the team than City, so the smart money was on them. Mancini planned otherwise, though, and made sure City were both tight defensively, but potent on the break and, with United unable to break through during their spell of dominance, City ran out winners – and, as it turned out, pretty easy winners, too.

The next game in the run – a 1-0 victory over Stoke in

the final – was definitely not one for the neutral. In fact, several non-City fans I know who watched the game thought the match was atrocious. But that wasn't important to the supporters. No, what mattered most was the result and who cared how City won their first trophy in three and a half decades? After all, it was understandable City were nervous – the fans in the stands were terrified they'd muck it up and that uneasiness often finds its way to the pitch.

Though while Mancini brought that memorable day for the fans, there was perhaps one indicator that suggested he wasn't as cool and calm as was originally thought. With Stoke coming into the game in the final few minutes – a series of corners needed dealing with, especially since Thomas Sorensen had joined the attack – and Silva had been sacrificed for the height of Vieira. He was City's calming influence on the pitch, coolly getting rid of the ball from the box and easing the pressure. Meanwhile, on the sidelines, Mancini was frantically waving his arms and screaming at his team. There was nothing calm there.

But that was Roberto Mancini, simply a man who wears his heart on his sleeve.

Though compare and contrast the two FA Cup finals he contested and the team's performances in them. Throughout the first, the club and its players were still relatively new to Mancini's methods. And, on that day against Stoke, the Blues were perhaps a little nervy at times, no more than you'd expect for a cup final, but they were certainly motivated. The same can't be said of the second, when City looked like they just couldn't get up for the game. It's not as if playing Wigan is that much different to playing Stoke; the Blues went into both finals as favourites.

The criticism was that Mancini had lost the dressing room, but again I'm not convinced that's fair on the Italian. To me, that would imply that his tactics and his football knowledge were below par, when clearly they weren't. If anything, he's probably one of the more forward thinking managers City have had in a long time. True, some of his formation tweaks and tactical play didn't work, but, for the most part, they did. It would probably be more accurate to say Mancini alienated the dressing room with his style of management – though, I'd hasten to say that's not much better than not being respected tactically.

When it came to the club's first title in 44 years, I'm willing to bet there will be none better. Having played some wonderful football for the first half of the season, but fallen to what seemed like an irreparable position, the fans had all but given up hope of the damage being undone. Slowly, it was clawed back and City went into the final day as favourites. The emotional rollercoaster surely peaked higher than any of the previous City years, while its drops and turns were sharper and more gut wrenching, too. From sheer despair to pure elation with the final kick of the season is something that will most likely never be bettered.

Without Roberto Mancini, that would probably have never been the case. Whether it was the manager's faults that hadn't helped with dips in form throughout the season is something we can only speculate about, but perhaps the odd poor tactical decision, the odd confrontation and the odd public outburst had led to the situation being as it was. Equally, there could have been the reverse influence too, as his actions may well have inspired the late resurgence.

Either way, Mancini delivered what will probably be remembered as City's best title ever, maybe even the best ending to a Premier League season, too. Needing two goals in stoppage time rather than just the one might could push it past the Liverpool-Arsenal game of 1989, though that had added spice since it was top versus second in a final day of the season showdown.

While his stints in Europe were unsuccessful with City,

Mancini almost performed well enough in the Premier League in his first half season to get the club into the top continental competition. In his three full seasons (minus two games of his last), he virtually strolled into the Champions League each year, securing automatic qualification into the groups as the Blues gate-crashed the top four for the first time.

In the competitions, he was dealt very difficult groups and was unlucky in his first attempt at qualification, given he secured enough points to have finished at least second in any of the other tables but the one the Blues were in. His next year was somewhat less successful, as City were the first English team eliminated without scoring a victory.

One of the biggest criticisms aimed at Mark Hughes during his time in the manager's office at Eastlands was that he spent money freely and badly. In some cases, it's difficult to argue against – for example, throwing £17.5m at Blackburn for Roque Santa Cruz was never going to be good business, as the striker had been suffering from injuries. And it was quickly proved so, as the Paraguayan failed to get a decent run in the team.

Equally, however, it's unfair to suggest that spending £25m on Emmanuel Adebayor was a bad move. The striker scored some crucial goals for the club and was part of a huge transitional period. It's impossible to sign players to jump straight from a mid-table outfit (in 2008-09) to title challengers. It does mean players will naturally be short term solutions as improvement is rapid, but there is a necessary step in the middle, of which Adebayor was crucial. Perhaps the fee was too high, but City's new status of 'richest club in the world' was always going to bump up the asking price, especially with financial fair play guidelines yet to be announced.

Perhaps Hughes' biggest problem with the players he signed was the contract lengths. He shouldn't be criticised for the signings he made, but for the long-term nature of their paperwork – the very fact that there are some of his signings whose contracts only expired at the end of the season Mancini lost his job is telling.

And just as those players were necessary to move the club on at the time, perhaps, when it comes to the bigger picture, sacking Mancini was a similar decision. It an was unpopular move, no question there, but not necessarily the wrong one. The best decisions are not always well received, after all, and there is a reason fans aren't involved in making such choices. My personal opinion would have been to give the Italian another season at least in charge of the club, but that's because I have the emotional attachment to the FA Cup win, the title in 2012, the 6-1 derby... the board don't. They have the best interests of the club at heart and they can see the effect he had on all the areas of Manchester City, both good and bad. Perhaps Mancini had taken the club as far as he could and maybe his management style was losing its effect, meaning he couldn't hit his own previous heights. Perhaps, quite simply, his negative points now outweighed his positives.

Whatever the down sides of his time with the club, though, Mancini did deserve at least some more dignity in his sacking. With rumours having leaked the night before the cup final, it put a huge dampener on his preparations and, no matter what anybody says about the professionalism of both players and managers, there will have been some effect on his work before the match.

Then having lost to Wigan, he was treated to a Sunday and Monday of speculation, before the news was confirmed in the evening. It's difficult to say what the club should have done. If they had denied the rumours and then relieved him of his duties, they were the bad guys for going against their word. If they didn't, as happened, then the silence spoke volumes as speculation grew and it became clear what the most likely outcome would be. They were in a lose-lose situation and chose the more professional approach to his sacking in not going back on their word – though perhaps the confirmation of the news could have come sooner, unless they had spoken to the manager himself privately a long while before the announcement was made.

Either way, for the distance he moved City forward and for the good times and success he brought the Blues, he didn't deserve to go in the manner he did. But that's football, and sometimes there are aspects clubs and people in the game can't control – not that he's the first City manager to have lost his job in embarrassing circumstances, of course. Mark Hughes had found out before his final game. Sven Goran Eriksson was the subject of a leak with two matches of the season and a post-season tour of Thailand to go.

Roberto Mancini Record

Overall
P189 **W**112 **D**38 **L**39 **F**356 **A**170
Win Rate: 59.26%

Premier League
P133 **W**82 **D**27 **L**24 **F**255 **A**110
Win Rate: 61.65%

European
P28 **W**13 **D**7 **L**8 **F**43 **A**29
Win Rate: 46.43%

Domestic Cups
P28 **W**17 **D**4 **L**7 **F**58 **A**31
Win Rate: 60.71%

And it's not as if Mancini didn't know it's a cut-throat world, given how he was introduced to the British press in his first media conference and how he'd seen his predecessor lose his job – he even said this was the case in that press conference.

Bizarrely, the very decision to sack Roberto Mancini will probably erase the bad aspects of his management from the history books as time goes on. When fans look back over eras of times gone by, they often do so with blue tinted spectacles. Only the best bits remain the most vivid, with the negatives slowly fading into insignificance. That Mancini lasted three and a half seasons at City, but won a league title, a domestic cup and the Community Shield, plus qualified for the Champions League group stages three times is what the fans will remember – and rightly so.

The good memories have been preserved before they can be sullied.

And Roberto Mancini should go down in history as the man who got Manchester City Football Club back onto the map. He pulled them back into the hunt for silverware. He raised their profile further and further each year. He made it exciting to be a Blue once again, as the good times far outweighed the bad and it's that which he deserves to be remembered for.

He was the man who restored pride to the club.